Recapturing the wonder of Christmas

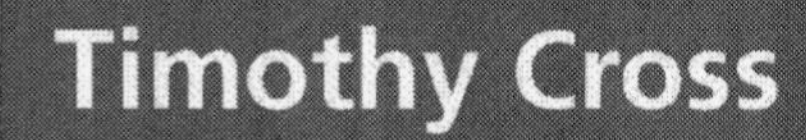
Timothy Cross

DayOne

ISBN 978-1-84625-657-8

British Library Cataloguing in Publication Data available

Published by Day One Publications
Ryelands Road, Leominster, HR6 8NZ
Telephone 01568 613 740 FAX 01568 611 473
email—sales@dayone.co.uk
web site—www.dayone.co.uk

Cover design by Kathryn Chedgzoy
Printed by 4Edge

One has become very conscious of a need in the Christian book world of a general introduction to and explanation of the subject of Christmas. A faithful presentation of the incarnation of our Saviour, Jesus Christ, is the need of the hour.

The trend in our current society is to remove all reference to any religious, let alone biblical basis to Christmas. 'Goodness, they are bringing religion into Christmas ... What next?' is a common feeling of a busy shopper on seeing a nativity scene in a shopping centre. This precious and warm celebration has become increasingly secular over the years. Few would deny that materialism has taken over almost completely.

The chapters which follow in this book seek to counter the current trend. They explain the true meaning of Christmas, and explore the different aspects we have come to believe and know about Christmas as committed Christians.

Whilst this book is definitely seasonal, its message is also eternal, for the purpose of the incarnation is eternal. 'You shall call his name Jesus, for he shall save his people from their sins.' The good news underlying Christmas is that when the Christmas experience actually happens *in* us, and the living Lord Jesus is known in our hearts, then the Christmas joy is not just seasonal but everlasting.

Veiled in flesh the Godhead see!
Hail, the incarnate Deity!

May this little book remind us of the eternal truths and lasting joys underlying Christmas.

Rev. Mark Pearce,
Saltmead Presbyterian Church,
Cardiff.

The wonder of Christmas

The first Christmas-time was a time when God became man. The wonder of Christmas is that in the incarnation of Christ, the infinite God actually came within the reach of finite men and women like you and me. In the virgin conception of Christ, and in his subsequent birth at Bethlehem nine months later, God actually took upon himself our humanity. In Christ, God became man. 1 Timothy 3:16 is an understatement when it says 'Great indeed, we confess, is the mystery of our religion: [God] was manifested in the flesh.'

I cannot remember a time when we didn't have a cat in our home. Our present cat is an affectionate, shy, tortoise-shell cat named Sally. Sally and I have gradually built a great rapport. We communicate with each other after a manner. She makes known to us when she is hungry or when she wants to go out. I think that I can even sense when she is smiling. She also understands me a little, especially when I use words like 'dish', 'bed' or 'down!' But whilst all this is true—and with respect to the Dr Doolittle cartoons I enjoyed as a boy, in which Dr Doolittle could actually talk to and be understood by animals—the gulf between me and our cat is very great. She is a cat and I am a human being.

If the gulf between us and our pets is great, what of the gulf between us and Almighty God? His awesome greatness is intimidating, and his holiness makes us afraid. We are finite, and he is infinite. We are very much flesh and blood, but 'God is Spirit' (John 4:24). We are characterised by weakness and dependence, but he is characterised by awesome power and total independence. We are sinners by nature, but he is immaculately and infinitely holy and pure. Truly, the gulf between the invisible God and us his creatures is very great.

Christ: the bringer of the revelation of God himself

The reality and wonder behind Christmas is that, in his grace and goodness, God has taken the initiative to bridge the gap between us and himself. He has done so by becoming man and being born at Bethlehem. In the Lord Jesus Christ we have the unsurpassed revelation of the one true God and, in the salvation he wrought at Calvary, we may know reconciliation to this God—if we put our trust in him.

In the Christ of Christmas we have the unsurpassed revelation of God because, as Matthew 1:23 tells us, Jesus is 'Emmanuel (which means, God with us)'. That this should ever have been so is a constant source of Christian praise, but especially so at Christmas, when Christians specifically ponder the wonder of the incarnation—that 'the Word became flesh and dwelt among us, full of grace and truth' (John 1:14). There is a hymn which articulates this praise:

Let earth and heaven combine,
Angels and men agree,
To praise in songs divine
The incarnate Deity,
Our God contracted to a span,
Incomprehensibly made man.

It is Jesus, then, who dispels our ignorance of God. He could say that 'He who has seen me has seen the Father' (John 14:9). Further, John 1:18 tells us, 'No one has ever seen God; the only Son who is in the bosom of the Father, he has made him known.'

Christ: the bringer of reconciliation to God himself

The Christ of Christmas bridges the gulf between us and our Maker particularly because he is the great reconciling Saviour as well as the great revealing Saviour. One of the ways in which the Bible describes salvation is in terms of reconciliation. It is Christ alone who can bring God and sinners together. The Christian gospel proclaims that 'in Christ God was reconciling the world to himself, not counting their trespasses against them' (2 Corinthians 5:19). In Christ, Christians have a joy which is peculiarly theirs: 'we rejoice in God through our Lord Jesus Christ, through whom we have now received our reconciliation' (Romans 5:11).

The bad news, though, precedes the good. The bad news is that it is our sin which cuts us off from our Maker. It is our sin which alienates us from him. It is our sin which makes us liable to the righteous anger of God—his wrath. But the Christ of Bethlehem was born with the specific purpose of reconciling alienated sinners to God. He did so thirty-three years later when he died on the cross of Calvary. On the cross, Christ took our sin and God's wrath upon Him, so that by believing in him we may be saved from God's wrath and reconciled to him for all eternity. 'Christ also died for sins once for all, the righteous for the unrighteous, that he might bring us to God' (1 Peter 3:18).

So do you know and rejoice in the Christ of Christmas? Have you realised that in Christ God actually became man, so that if we want to know what God is like, we need look no further than the Christ of the Bible? Do you also know that Jesus came into the world to reconcile God and sinners? Do you know that if you too believe in the babe of Bethlehem who grew up to become the Christ of Calvary, you also will know the joy and wonder of being at peace with your Maker for time and eternity?

Knowing the salvation wrought by the One who came at the first Christmas certainly gives us reason to celebrate!

Hark! the herald angels sing
Glory to the new-born King,
Peace on earth, and mercy mild,
God and sinners reconciled.
Joyful, all ye nations, rise,

Join the triumph of the skies;
With the angelic host proclaim,
'Christ is born in Bethlehem.'

Christ, by highest heaven adored,
Christ, the Everlasting Lord,
Late in time behold him come,
Offspring of a virgin's womb.
Veiled in flesh the Godhead see!
Hail the incarnate Deity!
Pleased as Man with men to dwell,
Jesus our Immanuel.

The joy of Christmas

Joy to the world! the Lord is come!
Let earth receive her King;
Let every heart prepare him room,
And heaven and nature sing.

Joy to the earth! the Saviour reigns!
Let men their songs employ;
While fields and floods, rocks, hills and plains,
Repeat the sounding joy.

Did you notice the emphasis on 'joy' in the lines just quoted? Sadly, I would say that there is very little true joy in our world today. There may be a temporary, frivolous mirth and happiness, but very little true and lasting joy. When we open the Bible, though—surprisingly for a book bound in black—we see that joy figures much in its pages, the first Christmas being no exception.

1. Imagine the joy of Mary and Joseph at the safe arrival of Jesus into the world. After travelling from Nazareth to Bethlehem, then having difficulty in finding their needed accommodation, their joy and relief at Jesus' birth must have been great. The joy was compounded by the knowledge that Mary had given birth to no ordinary baby, but to the Messiah—the eternal Son of God himself. Perhaps Mary employed the words of the 'Magnificat' once again: 'My soul magnifies the Lord, and my spirit rejoices in God my Saviour' (Luke 1:46–47). An angel had previously told Joseph 'You shall call his name Jesus, for he will save his people from their sins' (Matthew 1:21). Christians alone are privy to the unique joy of salvation—the joy of sins forgiven. Christmas was a vital

link in the chain of salvation—of God's plan of redemption. For Jesus was born to be our Saviour: he was born to die to procure the salvation of all who believe in him. He is the only Saviour. His birth was with a view to his death, his crib was with a view to his cross, his sacrifice was with a view to our eternal salvation.

2. Imagine the joy of those anonymous shepherds of Bethlehem. Shepherds in those days were somewhat despised: they were very low down on the social scale. But it was to some shepherds of Bethlehem that the heavenly announcement was made of 'good news of a great joy … for to you is born this day in the city of David a Saviour, who is Christ the Lord' (Luke 2:10–11). And so the shepherds went with haste to see the infant Christ. They were never the same again. Scripture records them returning to their occupation 'glorifying and praising God' (Luke 2:20).

It was fitting that shepherds should have been among the first to see the infant Christ. Jesus said of himself: 'I am the good shepherd. The good shepherd lays down his life for the sheep' (John 10:11). Paradoxically, Scripture also describes Jesus as the Lamb of God: 'Behold, the Lamb of God, who takes away the sin of the world' (John 1:29). 'Worthy is the Lamb who was slain' (Revelation 5:12).

3. Later on, as is well known, some wise men, or Magi, from Persia came to visit the infant Christ. Theirs was an arduous, long journey, but their exertions were repaid a thousandfold. They knew that Jesus was born to be King, and they just had to see him. Scripture records their joy. *They rejoiced exceedingly with great joy* (Matthew 2:10). Their journey reached its conclusion and climax when *they fell down and worshipped him* (Matthew 2:11). He alone is worthy.

4. The apostle Paul—one who knew Christ intimately, and whose life-long desire and ambition was that others would come to know him too—wrote this to some Christians in Philippi. *Rejoice in the Lord always; again I will say, Rejoice* (Philippians 4:4). Similarly, he closes his first letter to the Thessalonians with the injunction *Rejoice always, pray*

constantly, give thanks in all circumstances; for this is the will of God in Christ Jesus for you (1 Thessalonians 5:16–18).

It is a Christian duty then to be joyful. *Rejoice in the Lord always*. Isn't this an impossible command to obey, though? There is so much in our world and in our own lives to depress, discourage and drag us down ... The key is to note closely what Paul actually says. *Rejoice in the Lord:* 'in the Lord'. This reminds us of the unique and peculiar Christian joy which this world can neither give us nor take away from us. Rejoicing in the Lord—in the One born at Bethlehem, the One who died at Calvary—means rejoicing in his benefits. It is Christ alone who can bestow on us the gift of eternal life: pardon for sin, peace with God and the sure hope of a home in heaven by and by. In Christ alone we may know the true and eternal security so essential to our soul's true welfare.

Christmas, then, is to be a truly joy-full time for Christians. Yet the joy of the Lord which Christians know transcends the brief Christmas period which always seems to come and go so quickly. The blessing of God lasts for ever: hence our joy and praise, now and always. *Bless the LORD, O my soul, and forget not all his benefits* (Psalm 103:2). Joyful praise will be our eternal occupation. In praise, our joy in God's grace, our worship of him and our thanksgiving to him, although distinct, tend to get blended in one.

A happy Christmas? No. I wish you something better. I wish you the true and lasting joy of the Lord. For 'solid joys and lasting treasure, none but Zion's children know'.

My Saviour, thee possessing,
I have the joy, the balm,
The healing and the blessing,
The sunshine and the psalm;
The promise for the fearful,
The Elim for the faint;

The rainbow for the tearful,
The glory for the saint!

The wonder of a baby: the wonder of *the* baby

The birth of babies

The birth of a baby is always a wonderful event. Or is it? People talk about 'the miracle of life', but new life is not really miraculous, but normal; for women have been having babies ever since Adam's wife, Eve, gave birth to Cain and Abel.

Then there is the joy of child-birth—or is there? There is joy, and even relief, for the immediate family, but this joy will not be shared by strangers. Babies are no doubt being born at this very moment in Australia, but here in the UK we are carrying on unaffected.

Then think of some world famous figures—say Muhammad Ali, Billy Graham or the head of the United Nations. These figures were never honoured as babies, only as adults. What they have achieved in their prime is what interests and concerns us: we do not have pictures of them as babies.

The birth of *the* baby

When we bear the above in mind, and then consider the birth of Christ—that birth which underlies Christmas—we see that his birth is on an altogether different plane from any other birth. For a start, his birth has divided time into BC and AD. Also, his birth was truly miraculous, as the Bible teaches that Christ was conceived in the womb of the virgin Mary without the instrumentality of a human father. 'He was conceived by the power of the Holy Spirit, born of the Virgin Mary …' as the Apostles' Creed later put it.

The birth of Christ also affected far more than his immediate family.

In fact, the birth of Christ still affects millions. When we read the account of Christ's birth, though, we see some remarkable phenomena—phenomena which distinguish Christ's birth from all others.

1. When Christ was born at Bethlehem, the skies were suddenly filled with angelic praise: 'Glory to God in the highest, and on earth peace, good will among men' (Luke 2:14, RSV footnote). Here then was a birth vastly different from any other birth before or since. Here was a birth which actually elicited the praise of angels!

2. When Christ was born at Bethlehem, some humble shepherds in the nearby fields were told of it. They made their way to see the newly born baby, and after encountering him they were never the same again. Luke 2:20 relates how 'the shepherds returned, glorifying and praising God for all they had seen and heard'.

3. A little later on, when Jesus' parents brought him into the temple at Jerusalem, in obedience to the law, we meet a godly old gentleman by the name of Simeon—the only time we encounter this Simeon in the Bible. God had revealed to Simeon that he would not die until he had seen the promised Christ. Movingly, the Bible records that when Simeon saw the infant Christ 'he took him up in his arms and blessed God and said "Lord, now lettest thou thy servant depart in peace, according to thy word, for mine eyes have seen thy salvation ..."' (Luke 2:29–30).

4. Finally, when Jesus was born at Bethlehem, some Magi from Persia saw fit to make the long, arduous and hazardous journey to Israel to visit him. They knew that he was no ordinary child but the King of kings. On finding the infant Christ they honoured him accordingly. Matthew 2:11 records that 'they fell down and worshipped him'. Worship, of course, is due to God alone. Misplaced worship is idolatry. The Magi's worship of the infant Christ proves that here we are dealing with God: God in the flesh, Emmanuel, God with us.

So you can see that the birth of Christ was unusual. It affected and impacted people far beyond his immediate family. And the Christ born at Bethlehem still affects and impacts people's lives. Why? Luke 2:11 tells us why: 'To you is born this day in the city of David a Saviour, Who is Christ the Lord.'

The Christ of Bethlehem is the Saviour of the world. All have need of a Saviour, and in the Christ of Bethlehem—the same Christ who died at Calvary—we have God's own provision and remedy for our deepest need. 'Christ Jesus came into the world to save sinners' (1 Timothy 1:15). 'You shall call his name Jesus, for he will save his people from their sins' (Matthew 1:21).

The Christ born at Bethlehem, then, gives us all reason to be glad. For that baby was no ordinary baby, but God in the flesh—the One who alone can bestow eternal salvation: the forgiveness of sins and peace with God. Do you rejoice in the Christ of Bethlehem? You will only really do so if you are trusting in the same Christ who died for sinners at Calvary.

Sing, O sing this blessed morn!
Unto us a Child is born,
Unto us a Son is given,
God himself comes down from heaven.

God with us, Emmanuel,
Deigns for ever now to dwell;
He on Adam's fallen race
Sheds the fulness of his grace.

God comes down that man may rise,
Lifted by him to the skies;
Christ is Son of man that we
Sons of God in him may be.

Chapter 3

Sing, O sing, this blessed morn!
Jesus Christ today is born.

Bethlehem : Christmas 'on location'

One of my fantasies is to be able to celebrate Christmas in Bethlehem itself. Oh to be actually 'on location' at Christmas-time! I cannot see this happening in the immediate future, though, as (i) Such a fantasy would be rather pricey in reality and (ii) Bethlehem is currently caught up in the Arab-Israeli conflict, so going there any time might not be too advisable.

For this chapter, though, let us travel to Bethlehem in our mind's eye. Using the Bible as our guide we note:

1. Bethlehem's first mention

Bethlehem is first mentioned in the Bible in Genesis 35. Here it is the scene of both a sad and a happy event: namely the death of Rachel, Jacob's wife, as she gave birth to Benjamin. With her dying breath, Rachel named this child 'Ben-oni', meaning 'son of my sorrow'. Jacob, though, called his name 'Ben-jamin', meaning 'son of my right hand'. Jesus, who was also born in Bethlehem, in the fulness of time, paradoxically fulfils both of these names. He knew sorrow, for sure: he was 'Ben-oni', 'a man of sorrows, and acquainted with grief' (Isaiah 53:3). Yet now he is 'Ben-jamin', seated in glory 'at the right hand of the Majesty on high' (Hebrews 1:3).

2. The book of Ruth

The short book of Ruth, in the Old Testament, is also set in Bethlehem. The four chapters of this book comprise a very touching romance, in which we see the providence of God at work. The setting for the drama is the grain fields surrounding Bethlehem. Interestingly, the name

'Bethlehem' means 'House of Bread'. It was most fitting for Jesus to be born in this town, for he is the Bread of Life for our souls. He himself stated 'I am the bread of life; he who comes to me shall not hunger, and he who believes in me shall never thirst' (John 6:35).

3. Great David

1 Samuel 16 relates how David the shepherd was anointed king of Israel at Bethlehem. His anointing signified his being set apart for this high office, and being endowed with the Holy Spirit so that he could be enabled to live up to his high calling.

The Hebrew word for 'anointed one' is 'Messiah', and the Greek translation of Messiah is 'Christos' or 'Christ'. In the light of the whole Bible we know that Jesus is the longed for Messiah—the complete and total fulfilment of all the Old Testament hopes, prophecies, promises and aspirations. 'Hail to the Lord's anointed, great David's greater Son …' David—despite one or two glaring lapses—proved to be Israel's greatest earthly king. But the Bible describes Jesus as 'King of kings and Lord of lords' (Revelation 19:16)—in an infinitely higher category even than great David. One of Christ's three-fold offices is that of a King: 'Christ executeth the office of a King in subduing us to himself, in ruling and defending us and in restraining and conquering all his and our enemies' (*Westminster Shorter Catechism*).

4. The water of life

In 2 Samuel 23 there is a lesser known incident in which David expressed a longing to drink some of the water from the well at Bethlehem. David's 'mighty men' heeded David's desire and, putting their own lives at risk, went to draw some of the water from Bethlehem's well and brought it to David.

Water is vital for our life and well-being, of course. But what about the thirst of the soul? The Christ of Bethlehem is the answer to our need here. His invitation still stands: 'If any one thirst, let him come to me and drink. He who believes in me, as the scripture has said, "Out of his heart shall flow rivers of living water"' (John 7:37–38).

5. The fulfilment of prophecy

The Old Testament prophet Micah, in Micah 5:2, predicted the birth of Christ at Bethlehem, centuries before it actually occurred. The specific fulfilment of this prophecy shows how God always keeps his promises. Christ was certainly born in Bethlehem in the fulness of time. Mary and Joseph were resident in Nazareth in the north, but God's sovereign providence ensured that his Word was fulfilled. It was thus no accident when the expectant Mary and her husband Joseph made the arduous journey south to Bethlehem, and Jesus drew his first breath in the town for ever sanctified by his name. His birth at Bethlehem and his death at Calvary were all part of God's plan of redemption—a plan no natural or supernatural power could hinder or thwart.

6. The worship of the wise men

Matthew 2 records some wise men—or Magi—falling down and worshipping the infant Christ at Bethlehem. 'Going into the house they saw the child with Mary his mother, and they fell down and worshipped him ...' (Matthew 2:11). Worship belongs only to God. It is a basic biblical axiom that worshipping anyone or anything other than the one true God is committing the sin of idolatry. Scripture, though, here and elsewhere, records the worship belonging to God alone as given to Jesus. Scripture never condemns this 'Christolatry'. It goes to show that Jesus is the Son of God and God the Son—co-equal with the Father and the Holy Spirit in the mysterious unity of the Divine Trinity. Christianity is Christ and Jesus Christ is God. He was born at Bethlehem and he came into the world to save sinners like you and me.

Thank God, then, for the babe of Bethlehem, and thank God for the gospel of Christ. There is eternal hope for all who acknowledge their sin and put their faith in the One who was born at Bethlehem, who lived a sinless life, and then died an atoning death on Calvary's cross, to redeem us for all eternity.

O holy Child of Bethlehem,
Descend to us, we pray;
Cast out our sin, and enter in,
Be born in us today.
We hear the Christmas angels
The great glad tidings tell;
O come to us, abide with us,
Our Lord Emmanuel.

Christmas presents

If we were to ask the proverbial 'average schoolboy' what he likes most about Christmas, he would most likely give us a one-word answer: 'Presents!' If we were totally honest, we who have since left school might give this answer as well—but protocol demands that we are less than honest!

One wag once said, 'At Christmas, most parents spend more on their children than they did on the honeymoon that started it all.' Another, more dubious, character allegedly once muttered 'Only twenty-five shoplifting days to Christmas.'

Whilst there is no direct injunction in the Bible which orders us to give Christmas presents, it is yet appropriate and very much in-line with the spirit of the Bible to both give and receive presents at Christmas-time, for at the heart of Christmas is the greatest gift of all: 'God so loved the world that he gave his only Son that whoever believes in him should not perish but have eternal life' (John 3:16). In 2 Corinthians 9:15 Paul exclaims: 'Thanks be to God for his inexpressible gift!'—an exclamation which every Christian believer can echo sincerely.

So let us compare and contrast the Christmas presents which we give and receive with God's greatest present: the gift of eternal life in his Son.

Presents are free

Presents are free—if not, they cease to be presents. Imagine if someone gave you a lovely present, but the bill for it was attached for you to pay! Imagine that someone gave you a present, but the condition of its acceptance was that you did their shopping for them every week for the next year! Such again would cease to be a present: it would be a wage for services rendered.

God's gift of salvation comes to us freely, with no strings attached. Salvation is a gift to be received by faith. 'The free gift of God is eternal life in Christ Jesus our Lord' (Romans 6:23). Salvation by God's grace is one of the touchstones of biblical Christianity: 'it is the gift of God—not because of works, lest any man should boast' (Ephesians 2:8–9).

Presents cost

Whilst Christmas presents come to us freely—they are gifts—paradoxically, they also have to be paid for. They cost the giver something in time, thought, money and effort. And it is the same with salvation. Salvation is free, but it cost God's Son his very life-blood to procure our redemption. Jesus paid, and paid dearly for our salvation. 'You know that you were ransomed from the futile ways inherited from your fathers, not with perishable things such as silver or gold, but with the precious blood of Christ …' (1 Peter 1:18–19).

The guarantee

Gifts often come with a guarantee in their package. You can guarantee that if you receive a new watch which comes with a guarantee you will not have to pay for it to be mended if it breaks down for the first two years … it will stop working at midnight at the start of the third year!

God's Word, the Bible, is the guarantee of God's goodwill towards us, and the guarantee of the eternal security of the soul which belongs to Jesus. The Bible contains the promises of a God who cannot lie. God keeps his word. God's Word is totally dependable. Christians have the 'hope of eternal life which God, who never lies, promised ages ago …' (Titus 1:2).

The instructions

Gifts often come with an instruction booklet or manual: what we are to do and what we are not to do with our present. We do well to heed these instructions, as the manufacturer knows the product best.

Similarly, the Bible may be considered as God our Maker's instruction manual to us. Our Maker knows best! We will do well to heed his Word if we desire a happy life, a happy death and a happy eternity. 'This book of the law shall not depart out of your mouth, but you shall meditate on it day and night, that you may be careful to do according to all that is written in it; for then you shall make your way prosperous, and then you shall have good success' (Joshua 1:8).

Just what I needed!

A good present is a suitable present, tailor-made for us. Those closest to us know our interests, quirks and fancies. They don't want to waste money and give us something we don't want or will not use.

God knows only too well our need of a Saviour. We are sinners who need to be saved. In giving his Son, God provided the Saviour we so desperately need. 'You shall call his name Jesus, for he will save his people from their sins' (Matthew 1:21). It was on the cross that Jesus procured the salvation of his people, shedding his precious blood for the forgiveness of their sins. The manger of Bethlehem was with a view to the cross of Calvary, which was with a view to securing the eternal salvation of God's people. Jesus saves!

A special present

Lastly, a good present is special and out of the ordinary—it even makes us gasp somewhat. In giving his own Son, God gave the best that heaven had and the best that you and I can ever have. In Jesus, all who believe have the gift of eternal life: the forgiveness of sins, peace with God and a glorious home in heaven guaranteed. God's gift of eternal life is the greatest gift we can ever receive. It cannot be bought. It is a gift which this world can neither give nor take away. It is a gift which may be enjoyed in this life as well as the next, and it is a gift which alone gives eternally lasting joy to its receiver.

So the big question is: Have you received this greatest of gifts? Have you received the Lord Jesus Christ as your own, personal Saviour? 'To all who received him, who believed in his name, he gave power to become children of God' (John 1:12).

'Thanks be to God for his inexpressible gift!' (2 Corinthians 9:15).

Christmas decorations

Some of us find Christmas decorations quite exciting. In early December in my home city of Cardiff, great ceremony is made of the switching on of the Christmas lights in the city centre. Observing this brings back some early memories of the Blackpool illuminations. Then there is a certain house in the road where my younger brother used to live. Its Christmas decorations, both within, without and even on the chimney are so lavish that it has become something of a local tourist attraction. They even have a wishing-well in the garden, into which observers can throw coins to donate to local charities. Christmas-time often finds me posting leaflets through house doors: leaflets which give details of planned church services. The Christmas decorations of some homes grab attention. Some have lights inside and out. Others have a strange mix of artefacts, where a mythical figure like a jolly Father Christmas seems to be put on the same level as the historical figures of Mary, Joseph and the shepherds of Bethlehem. So much, then, for Christmas decorations. They add colour to the dark winter, even if taking them down once Christmas is over is a rather tedious occupation.

A house which looks pretty and attractively decorated to the eye, however, is not necessarily the whole story. How many of the homes which I leaflet are going through stress and strain? How many are suffering from marital tension or even divorce? How many contain children who rebel and cause their parents trouble and sorrow? Then there are the uncertainties of this world, such as the hidden fears of not being able to make ends meet, or of having to battle against ill-health. Outward appearances can deceive. Bright decorations can mask the darkness of heart and spirit which many people feel acutely.

God knows

In 1 Samuel 16:7 we read 'The LORD sees not as man sees; man looks on the outward appearance, but the LORD looks on the heart.' The God of the Bible sees and knows us as we really are. He can see through and beyond our external style, make-up and façade. He can look beyond the impressions we give to others and the roles which we play and play-act. 'O LORD, thou hast searched me and known me! … Thou discernest my thoughts from afar (Psalm 139:1–2).

God loves

The message of Christmas is the good news that God loves and cares about us enough to deliver us from the root cause of all our inner misery. At the first Christmas, God in Christ came to change us from the inside out. The Bible says that we are sinners by nature and practice. 'If we say we have no sin, we deceive ourselves, and the truth is not in us' (1 John 1:8). It is our sin which mars our relationship with God, and it is our sin which is the root cause of all the misery and disharmony in the world. The law of God has been replaced by the anarchy of hell. Joy and contentment in God have been replaced by a manic seeking for satisfaction in the passing things of this life. When we are away from the love and light of God, we can only expect tension, darkness and misery, and eternal judgement if we die unrepentant and without saving faith in Christ.

'I am this dark world's light'

Hear again the good news of the Christmas gospel. John 1:9 tells us, 'The true light that enlightens every man was coming into the world.' 2 Corinthians 5:19 tells us that 'in Christ God was reconciling the world to himself, not counting their trespasses against them'. In Jesus there is salvation from sin, reconciliation to God and the healing of our inner selves made sick by sin. Just as a sick person welcomes the visit of the doctor, how much more should we welcome Jesus into our hearts. He receives sinners. He saves sinners. He reconciles sinners to God. He puts us together again. He said of himself in Mark 2:17: 'Those who are well have no need of a physician, but those who are sick; I came not to call the righteous, but sinners.'

Jesus, then, is the Saviour that this world so desperately needs. The babe of Bethlehem grew up, and after living a sinless life, offered himself up as an atoning sacrifice on behalf of sinners on Calvary's cross. When we trust the crucified Saviour, our sins are forgiven, our relationship with God is restored, and we are assured of a home in heaven: a home eternally free from all that brings us down in this life.

Take heed!

Be careful, then, not to get distracted or even dazzled by the externals of Christmas. Keep the Lord Jesus Christ central. May the Christmas lights remind you that Jesus is the Light of the world (John 8:12). May the gifts you give and receive remind you of God's great gift of his Son. May the Christmas tree remind you of the One who, 1 Peter 2:24 tells us, 'himself bore our sins in his body on the tree'. Jesus died to redeem us from sin and its consequent misery. It is Jesus who is the reason for the season.

Hark, the glad sound! the Saviour comes,
The Saviour promised long;
Let every heart exult with joy
And every voice be song

He comes the broken heart to bind,
The bleeding soul to cure,
And with the treasures of his grace
To enrich the humble poor.

Chapter 6

The Christmas tree

Brightly coloured Christmas trees, either real or imitation, have figured prominently in a typical European Christmas for a long time. The large Christmas tree which graces Trafalgar Square in London each year is an annual goodwill gift from Norway. Then in my home village north of Cardiff each year we enjoy a 'carols around the Christmas tree' evening in the village square. The atmosphere for this is always festive, with the Salvation Army band, the large crowd all wrapped up against the elements, and the ceremonial decorating of the tree and the turning on of the lights.

Christmas trees, though, are not to everyone's taste. A Christian friend of mine is adamant that Christmas trees are of pagan origin, and so are to be shunned rather than welcomed. He cites God's rebuke to Israel in Jeremiah 2:20: 'under every green tree you bowed down as a harlot'.

The true Christmas tree

Whilst there is no direct biblical sanction for having a Christmas tree, it is also not inappropriate for trees to figure in our Christmas celebrations, because at the heart of the Christian faith there lies a tree. The cross of Christ—his redeeming work at Calvary—is the centre of the Christian gospel. Five times in the New Testament the cross of Christ is referred to as a 'tree'. For example: 'They put him to death by hanging him on a tree' (Acts 10:39).

The word 'tree' was a highly significant and 'loaded' one for the writers of the New Testament. In Galatians 3:13, Paul, quoting from Deuteronomy 21, explained: 'Christ redeemed us from the curse of the law, having become a curse for us—for it is written, 'Cursed be every one who hangs on a tree'. For the New Testament writers, steeped in their

Old Testament background as they were, the word 'tree' was synonymous with God's curse: his judgement on sin, and his punishment for breaking his law. God had pronounced to Moses: 'If a man has committed a crime punishable by death ... and you hang him on a tree ... a hanged man is accursed by God' (Deuteronomy 21:22–23).

The 'tree', then, unlocks the meaning of the death of Christ. It tells us that Christ was actually cursed by God when he died at Calvary in the sinner's place—cursed that we might be blessed. He suffered the punishment of God upon sin so that by believing in him we might know the pardon of God for our sin. He was condemned that we might be justified. Because of his suffering, 'There is therefore now no condemnation for those who are in Christ Jesus' (Romans 8:1):

Death and the curse were in our cup;
O Christ, 'twas full for thee;
But thou hast drained the last dark drop,
'Tis empty now for me.
That bitter cup, love drank it up;
Now blessing's draught for me.

Christmas tree fairies?

A less than happy feature of Christmas trees, from a Christian perspective, is the fairy which sometimes stands on the top of them. But here we can learn by contrast. Fairies are mythological. They are not real. They exist in the world of make-believe, but not in reality. The Christmas story, though, is true. Any honest reading of the Gospel records—records written in such a plain, unembellished way—will convince the reader that in dealing with the Christ of Bethlehem, we are dealing with fact not fiction: God's truth, not man's tale. The Christian faith is a historical faith. It is based on facts which occurred in time and space, in the land of

Israel in the first century. We confirm the reality of Christmas every time we write the date, for Christ's birth divided time into BC and AD. The facts of Christ's birth, ministry, death and resurrection are facts of sober history, not invented mythology. He is a real Saviour who really saves!

Christmas tree lights

An agreeable feature of Christmas trees is the lights which sometimes adorn their branches. How the Christmas tree lights add cheer to a dark winter evening! In Bible times—well before the advent of the electric light bulb—there was much fear of darkness. Darkness spoke of danger and the terror of the unknown. In the Bible, darkness also speaks of the wrath of God, for hell—the ultimate in God's judgement—is described as 'the outer darkness' (Matthew 8:12 et al.). Light, then, is necessary for both physical and spiritual life and well-being. Light is necessary to dispel the darkness, and all that darkness brings and means.

It is against this background that we recall Jesus' affirmation, 'I am the light of the world; he who follows me will not walk in darkness, but will have the light of life' (John 8:12). At Calvary, for three hours, Jesus suffered the darkness of God's judgement on sin, so that we might become the children of light. When we believe in him we are delivered from the dominion of darkness, and will one day bask in God's radiant light for evermore. Because of Jesus, the Christian's future is brighter than bright! In glory, darkness will be banished eternally, for there the 'night shall be no more' (Revelation 22:5).

Presents!

Lastly, it is traditional in many homes to place our carefully-wrapped Christmas presents for one another at the base of the Christmas tree. The presents around the Christmas tree may remind us once again that salvation too is a gift to receive, and not something which we work to achieve on the basis of what we do or are. Salvation by God's grace—his undeserved kindness to the undeserving and ill-deserving—is the hallmark of biblical Christianity. 'The free gift of God is eternal life in Christ Jesus our Lord' (Romans 6:23). 'It is the gift of God—not because of works, lest any man should boast (Ephesians 2:8–9).

Should or shouldn't a Christian have a Christmas tree in their home at Christmas time? Different Christians have different views. Perhaps it is best to agree to disagree. 'Let every one be fully convinced in his own mind' (Romans 14:5). But whilst Christians may have differing opinions on whether or not we should have a Christmas tree, on the question of 'the Tree' all Christians are in complete unity and concord. All Christians can testify with joy that 'he himself bore our sins in his body on the tree (1 Peter 2:24), for the tree of Calvary and its significance and saving potency lie at the heart of the heart of Biblical Christianity.

O tree of glory, tree most fair,
Ordained those holy limbs to bear,
How bright in purple robe it stood—
The purple of a Saviour's blood.

Upon its arms, like balance true,
He weighed the price for sinners due,
The price which none but he could pay,
And spoiled the spoiler of his prey

To thee, eternal Three in One,
Let homage meet by all be done;
As by the Cross thou dost restore,
So rule and guide us evermore.

Where is the host?

If you played that word association game and mentioned the word 'Christmas', most people would conjure up the word 'celebration'. Talking of celebrations, I once heard of a fellow who gave a huge party for his family and friends to celebrate his retirement. He hired a hall, outside caterers, a band and a sound system and then sent out over a hundred invitations to various friends and associates to come to his special party, on the first Saturday after he had retired from work. The hordes duly arrived, and they really whooped it up. The strange thing was, though, that at the last minute, the host got a touch of depression. All sorts of morbid thoughts about growing old and being of no more use in life began to fill his mind. These thoughts weighed so heavily upon him that he just didn't feel in the mood to attend the party which he had given, and so he stayed at home. Yet funnily, the host's absence did not stop everyone else from having a good time! They enjoyed the camaraderie, had a good feast on the free food, and the more extrovert danced away to the music. No one seemed to notice that the host was missing. The very purpose of the party got drowned in all the hype and celebration.

Before we laugh at those party-goers, though, isn't that precisely the danger with Christmas? We can get so swamped and caught up in the celebrations that we forget what we are actually celebrating. We forget the host of the party, the Lord Jesus Christ himself.

How do we avoid forgetting what Christmas is all about? We do so by constantly recalling the original Christmas message. This message was beamed from heaven to earth by an angel to some shepherds in a field. They were ordinary people, for sure, but on grasping the message sent to them they were filled with the most extraordinary joy and praise. We can be too. The original Christmas message is contained in Luke 2:11: 'to you is born this day in the city of David a Saviour, who is Christ the Lord'. Unpacking this message, notice four points:

1. The place

The Christmas message is bound up with a real place in time and space, namely Bethlehem, 'the city of David'. From this we can see that Christmas is no fantasy or make-believe, like Santa Claus and the fairy on the tree. No. The first Christmas was a real event in time and space some two thousand years ago, when God became man in Jesus Christ and was born in Bethlehem. The city of David—the birthplace of Israel's greatest earthly king—was graced by the visit of 'great David's greater Son', and all in exact fulfilment of the promises God had made. No wonder the heavens started to sing! God had descended to earth in Christ, so that every believer might eventually ascend at last to heaven.

2. The person

Notice secondly that Christmas is bound up with a Person as well as a place. Christmas concerns no ordinary person, but 'Christ the Lord'. Herein lies the uniqueness and incomparability of Christmas. That baby born in Bethlehem was not merely man, but the Christ—God's anointed One, the longed for prophet, priest and king. And Christ is 'the Lord', that is, God himself in human flesh. So, paradoxically, what a serious and solemn—as well as joyful—celebration Christmas is. This is no human party, as here we are celebrating what God himself has done in entering our sordid world of time and space. At Christmas we may rejoice that the God who created everything cares for us and loves us so much that he actually chose to reveal himself to us in the best possible way—by becoming one of us.

Christ the Lord. What a Person! How fitting is the invitation, 'Come, let us adore him.' 'Lord' is a title of deity. The Son of God became a son of man that the sons of men might become the sons of God.

3. The purpose

Notice thirdly that the original Christmas message reveals a purpose. 'To you is born this day in the city of David a *Saviour.*' The name 'Jesus' means 'Saviour'. 'You shall call his name Jesus, for he will save his people from their sins' (Matthew 1:21).

Knowing Christ as our own personal Saviour is basic to Christianity. The Bible is crystal clear that the purpose of Jesus being born was to be our Saviour—to die on a cross, and so pay the death penalty which we owe for our sins. At Calvary, God judged Jesus so that he might extend mercy to us. 'Christ died for our sins' (1 Corinthians 15:3). Most of us are born to live, not die, and normally we hope to live as long as possible. Yet God ordained that Jesus was born to die. And Jesus achieved far more by his death than his life, as it was by his death that he procured the redemption of his people. It was by his death that he gave his life as a ransom for many.

Of course, we will only trust in Jesus as our Saviour if we see that we have a desperate need of him, and that we actually need saving. It is only when we are convinced that we are guilty, condemned sinners in the sight of God that we will cling to the life-raft, and cry out 'Lord Jesus, save me.' It is because many are deluded into thinking that they are all right as they are, that they do not trust in Jesus as their Saviour, and think of Jesus, if at all, solely as a teacher, a moral leader, a carpenter, or a baby to sing carols about. But all who do come to realise their need of a Saviour will find in Jesus the all-sufficient Saviour for their need.

4. The pertinence

Christmas is and always will be highly pertinent and relevant, for the message of Christmas concerning God's Son and the provision of a Saviour is addressed *to you*—just as much as it was originally addressed to those anonymous shepherds of Bethlehem.

No doubt you will receive a few presents at Christmas time,

tailor-made, given to you and received gratefully by you. But what about God's gift of his Son? Jesus is the original, perfect and lasting Christmas present—a gift wrapped in swaddling cloths.

The Bible reveals a God who is loving and giving. 'God so loved the world that he gave his only Son that whoever believes in him should not perish but have eternal life' (John 3:16). Gifts are for receiving, and believing is receiving, for 'to all who received him [Jesus], who believed in his name, he gave power to become children of God' (John 1:12).

A truly happy Christmas, then, is a Christ-centred Christmas—receiving and enjoying God's best—the Saviour who is Christ the Lord.

The first Christmas rush

I don't know about you, but it seems to me that Christmas begins earlier and earlier as the years go by. In my home city of Cardiff, at any rate, the Christmas lights are up by the end of November. I can also recall that when I was in college, I attended a Christmas carol service as early as December 4th. The Christmas bustle and 'rush' gains its momentum weeks before the day itself.

For this chapter, I should like us to consider what has been termed 'the first Christmas rush'. It concerns those shepherds who were 'out in the field, keeping watch over their flock by night' (Luke 2:8) on the first Christmas. Their story is well known. The angel of the Lord appeared to them and told them the 'good news of a great joy ... a Saviour who is Christ the Lord' (Luke 2:10–11). The shepherds took heed, believed the promise, and 'voted with their feet'. For they said to each other 'Let us go over to Bethlehem and see this thing that has happened ...' (Luke 2:15). And then Luke 2:16 records the first Christmas rush, for we read 'And they went *with haste*, and found Mary and Joseph, and the babe lying in a manger.'

The first Christmas rush? Most definitely—and yet a very different rush from today's Christmas rush: a rush that all too often results in financial debt. The first Christmas rush was a rush to see the infant Christ:

Who is he in yonder stall,
At whose feet the shepherds fall?

'Tis the Lord! O wondrous story!
'Tis the Lord, the King of glory!

At his feet we humbly fall;
Crown him, crown him Lord of all.

The grace of God

The whole of the incident concerning the shepherds of Bethlehem is another instance of the amazing grace of God. Why were shepherds the first visitors to see the Messiah? Why not people of worldly importance, such as scribes, Pharisees or kings? Shepherds were considered the outcasts of society in Bible days. Their work kept them away from the temple for weeks on end, so they were unable to attain ceremonial cleanness. They also lived a very humble lifestyle—only managing to stay slightly above the poverty line. Yet it was to such men that the good news of the gospel came: the good news of 'a Saviour who is Christ the Lord'.

Shepherds and sheep. How ironic! The Jesus whom the shepherds worshipped is actually both. He said of himself, 'I am the good shepherd. The good shepherd lays down his life for the sheep' (John 10:11). And John the Baptist pointed to Jesus and said 'Behold, the Lamb of God, who takes away the sin of the world' (John 1:29).

The shepherds of Bethlehem. By this world's reckoning they were poor outcasts—but the Bible shows that they were the recipients of the grace of God! Such is often the case. The proud and self-sufficient often are unable to realise their need of God and their need of salvation. The Bible can often seem topsy-turvy when judged by this world's yardstick. In Luke 1:51–53 we read: 'he has scattered the proud in the imagination of their hearts, he has put down the mighty from their thrones, and exalted those of low degree; he has filled the hungry with good things, and the rich he has sent empty away'. Then in 1 Corinthians 1:27–29 we read that 'God chose what is foolish in the world to shame the wise, God chose what is weak in the world to shame the strong, God chose what is low and despised in the world, even things that are not, to bring to nothing things that are, so that no human being may boast in the presence of God'.

The shepherds would have said 'Amen' to the verses just cited. Scripture records how, after seeing the baby Jesus, 'the shepherds returned, glorifying and praising God for all they had heard and seen, as it had been told them' (Luke 2:20). They glorified and praised God! In doing so, they were doing the work of the angels: a few lines earlier Luke had recorded 'a multitude of the heavenly host praising God and saying "Glory to God in the highest, and on earth peace, good will among men"' (Luke 2:13–14, RSV footnote).

Praising God: our highest occupation

In glorifying and praising God, the shepherds reached the summit of human existence and fulfilment this side of the grave. The *Westminster Shorter Catechism* reminds us that 'Man's chief end is to glorify God and to enjoy him for ever.' The shepherds praised God in response to his favour and goodwill to them—just as those who have received Christ as their Saviour have done for the past two thousand years and continue to do.

But what did the shepherds do next? They returned. That is, they went back to their jobs—the same old routine, if you like. Yet it was not the same old routine. They were now new men, going back to the same old job. And this holds true today. Thank God that he is the God of the ordinary as well as the spectacular. It is nice to enjoy Christmas, but thank God that the cheer of the gospel does not end when the Christmas season ends. If we are Christians, we may enjoy the presence of God at Christmas, but also in the cold of January and February, when we go back to work in the sleet, and when we catch the flu, and through all the disappointments and setbacks which are sure to beset us in the year ahead. Jesus is an all-year-round Friend and Saviour. He is in fact a Friend for all seasons and a Friend for all eternity. He is as worthy of our trust as he is worthy of our praise.

Chapter 9

Hark, the glad sound! the Saviour comes,
The Saviour promised long;
Let every heart prepare a throne,
And every voice a song

He comes the broken heart to bind,
The bleeding soul to cure,
And with the treasures of his grace
To enrich the humble poor.

'In loving-kindness, Jesus came ...'

In loving-kindness, Jesus came
My soul in mercy to reclaim ...

Whilst the above lines are not actually taken from a Christmas carol, their sentiments exactly encapsulate the meaning of Christmas.

Like most, I enjoy the outward trappings of Christmas a great deal: Santa, tinsel, lights, mince pies, days off, etc. Yet these, agreeable though they are, have no real connection with the Christ of the Bible whose birth underlies the real reason to celebrate Christmas.

It should be no more necessary to talk of a Christian Christmas than it is to talk of a round circle. But with so many 'Christmas distractions', it is always good to remind ourselves that the heart of Christmas is the coming of Christ into the world. The incarnation—that epochal time when God became man and walked on our planet—is the essence of what Christmas is really all about.

In Galatians 4:4 we read: 'when the time had fully come, God sent forth his son, born of woman'. Returning 'back to basics', then, and focusing/ refocusing on the Christ born at Bethlehem, let us consider both the pre-existence of his being and the purpose of his coming.

1. The pre-existence of his being

'God sent forth his Son ...' To be sent, Christ had to exist already. According to the Bible, Bethlehem was not Christ's actual beginning, but just a change in his mode of existence. According to the Bible, Christ had no beginning. He is eternal. He existed before he was born. He is as eternal as God is eternal, for in eternity past he lived in the unity of love which characterizes the three Persons of the One God, Father, Son and Holy Spirit (the doctrine of the Trinity is one of the bedrocks of orthodox Christianity).

Eternity is a characteristic of God. So Christ's eternal pre-existence is one proof that in dealing with Jesus we are dealing with God himself. The Lord Jesus was aware of his own pre-existence, as in his famous 'high priestly prayer' to his Father in John 17, he mentioned 'the glory which I had with thee before the world was made' (John 17:5).

John's Gospel opens with a staggering statement concerning Christ's pre-existence. John 1:1–2 sets the backcloth to all that follows when it declares, 'In the beginning was the Word, and the Word was with God, and the Word was God. He was in the beginning with God.'

Only an eternal One could save us eternally—and such a One is Christ. We must be careful not to go with the crowd and over-sentimentalise the babe of Bethlehem. For, as the hymn says:

Lo, within a manger lies
He who built the starry skies.

Secondly though, consider:

2. The purpose of his coming

The Bible leaves us in no doubt as to the purpose behind Christ's coming into the world. 1 Timothy 1:15 states succinctly: *Christ Jesus came into the world to save sinners*. That is, he came to save us from the dreadful penalty which we ought to pay because we have sinned against God. Strange but true, Christmas was with a view to Easter. Christ's birth was with a view to his death. His cradle was with a view to his cross. For it was on the cross of Calvary that Christ died as an eternal sacrifice for sinners. It was at Calvary that he shed his precious blood for the sinner's pardon. It was at Calvary that he died so that we might have eternal life.

In John 10:10 Jesus stated the purpose of his coming this way: 'I came that they might have life, and have it abundantly.' The Bible would have us distinguish between existing and truly living life with a capital 'L'. Not everyone who is alive and physically well has eternal life. Eternal life is a synonym for salvation. Eternal life is the life of God in the soul of man. Eternal life may be gained and enjoyed only through trusting the babe of Bethlehem who became the Saviour of Calvary. 'The free gift of God is eternal life in Christ Jesus our Lord' (Romans 6:23). What do we have to do to enjoy this gift of eternal life? We do not actually have to do anything, as it is what it says—it is indeed a free gift.

Consider finally another of Jesus' own explanations of his coming, as detailed in Mark 2:17. There he tells us 'I came not to call the righteous, but sinners.' So the way to receive and enjoy the gift of eternal life is just to admit our sin and need, and cast ourselves wholly on the Christ who came to save and call sinners to himself. The good news is that Jesus has never refused any one yet. 'Him who comes to me I will not cast out' (John 6:37). He is the Friend and Saviour of needy, undeserving and ill-deserving sinners.

Yes, Jesus Christ is God. As such he always existed. But at the first Christmas, God in Christ was born, so that we might be blessed beyond all blessing. So the big question, looking beyond the Christmas trappings, is: 'Do you know the eternal blessing of God in Christ?'

Yea, Lord, we greet Thee,
Born for our salvation;
Jesus, to thee be glory given;
Word of the Father,
Now in flesh appearing:
O come, let us adore him,
Christ the Lord!

'I'm dreaming of a white Christmas'

Every Christmas-time, two things seem rather predictable. (i) Bing Crosby's record 'I'm dreaming of a white Christmas' will be played rather frequently over the radio or the supermarket sound system; and (ii) the weather men will tell us the likelihood of having snow on Christmas Day—the likelihood of 'a white Christmas'. Like most, I have mixed feelings about a truly white Christmas-that is, a covering of a few inches of snow, as opposed to a few flakes in the air which don't settle. Yes, a covering of snow looks pretty, and seems to dampen down the sound, giving a lovely stillness. But when sentimentality is replaced by practicality, snow can be rather inconvenient, making it more difficult to travel to work or to see relatives. The occasional fall of deep snow seems to bring the UK to a grinding halt.

As a reader of the Bible, I notice that snow features occasionally in its pages too. Snow is used in Scripture as 'picture language' to describe three fundamental truths: truths pertinent to us all. The three truths are these: God's peerless splendour, our pitiful state, and our perfect salvation.

1. God's peerless splendour

The Bible declares that 'God is light and in him is no darkness at all' (1 John 1:5). This refers to the awesome purity of God in his very being—a purity beyond our comprehension. Daniel, in his vision of God, describes him in the best way in which our limited vocabulary can: 'His raiment was white as snow, and the hair of his head like pure wool' (Daniel 7:9). Then, in the last book of the Bible, John literally fell over when he glimpsed the Lord Jesus in his risen, ascended and glorified splendour: 'His head and his hair were white as white wool, white as snow; his eyes were like a flame of fire' (Revelation 1:14).

Here our dilemma begins. We are all made to know and love God, but when we sense his dazzling splendour and holiness, understandably we are afraid and shrink back. The brightness of the divine 'snow' makes the blackness of our sin stand out that much more starkly; which leads us to:

2. Our pitiful state

A covering of snow can look lovely and picturesque. But if you dig below the surface what will you find? Alas, soil, dirt and even rubbish. Isn't that just like us? We may of course hide and cover over our true inner selves, and fool those around us. But our rotten inside is not hidden from God. The Bible says, 'The LORD sees not as man sees; man looks on the outward appearance, but the LORD looks on the heart' (1 Samuel 16:7). 'Before him no creature is hidden, but all are open and laid bare to the eyes of him with whom we have to do' (Hebrews 4: 13).

Our inward state is such that by nature we are unfit for fellowship with a thrice-holy God. When we are enabled to realise this, we may employ the words of David in Psalm 51. At the time when David wrote Psalm 51, having lapsed into adultery, and suffering the pangs of conscience resulting from this act, he cried out vehemently to God. Aware of the pollution of his nature, he prayed, 'Create in me a clean heart, O God … Purge me with hyssop, and I shall be clean; wash me, and I shall be whiter than snow' (Psalm 51:10,7). Sadly, by nature our state is one of sinful, inner defilement. But there is a gospel! There is a way in which sinners can be cleansed from the stain of sin and made as white as snow in God's sight:

3. Perfect salvation

The lengthiest prophecy in the Bible is the prophecy of Isaiah. Isaiah's prophecy consists of a formidable sixty-six chapters. But Isaiah—whose name means 'The Lord delivers'—opens his prophecy with a gospel invitation. Yes, he pulls no punches as to the sinner's state which makes this gospel such a necessity—'Ah sinful nation, a people laden with iniquity …' (Isaiah 1:4)—but then, still in the very first chapter of his prophecy, God through Isaiah gives the glorious invitation: 'Come now, let us reason together, says the LORD: though your sins are like scarlet, they shall be as white as snow; though they are red like crimson, they shall become like wool' (Isaiah 1:18).

There is a gospel of purification, then. There is a way in which unclean sinners can be cleansed. The Bible tells us that 'the blood of Jesus his Son cleanses us from all sin' (1 John 1:7). The potency of the blood of Jesus is such that it makes unclean sinners fit for heaven! Revelation 7:14 describes the inhabitants of heaven, not in terms of their own merit, but solely in terms of the soul-cleansing merits of the blood of Jesus: 'They have washed their robes and made them white in the blood of the Lamb.'

Will it or won't it be a 'white Christmas' this year? It's never certain that it will be. Next time you see the snow, though, either for real or in a picture, give thanks for the gospel of the Lord Jesus Christ which underlies the Christmas celebrations. The One born at Bethlehem shed his blood for sinners at Calvary. And the blood of Jesus washes unclean sinners whiter even than the snow. The Bible tells us so.

What can wash away my stain?
Nothing but the blood of Jesus;
What can make me whole again?
Nothing but the blood of Jesus.

Oh! precious is the flow
That makes me white as snow;

No other fount I know,
Nothing but the blood of Jesus.

For my cleansing this I see—
Nothing but the blood of Jesus;
For my pardon this my plea—
Nothing but the blood of Jesus.

Oh! precious is the flow
That makes me white as snow;
No other fount I know,
Nothing but the blood of Jesus.

No vacancies

There is a guesthouse in my favourite seaside resort which has had a permanent 'No Vacancies' sign up in its window for at least the last two years. If you did not know otherwise, you would think that they are constantly full of guests. I know, though, that the proprietors are having some time out from the bed and breakfast business. Rather than giving the impression of closing down completely, they consider that the 'No Vacancies' option is the best one whilst they regroup.

It is very well known that there were 'no vacancies' at the first Christmas time. Luke records how Mary *gave birth to her first-born son, and wrapped him in swaddling cloths, and laid him in a manger, because there was no place for them in the inn* (Luke 2:7).

Picture the stress and distress which Joseph and Mary must have experienced at that time. They had made the compulsory long journey from Nazareth to Bethlehem in the days when air-conditioned coaches had not been thought of. Mary was in the latter stages of pregnancy. On arriving in Bethlehem, to their shock, the 'No Vacancies' signs, as it were, were up everywhere. You can imagine Joseph pleading with an innkeeper: 'Please help. My wife is expecting a baby any moment.' Eventually, one anonymous person did what he could with what he had. He said that they could lodge in his animal shelter—at least it was warm and dry. And it was in that animal shelter that no less than the eternal Son of God was born and so '[God] was manifested in the flesh' (1 Timothy 3:16).

Who is he in yonder stall,
At whose feet the shepherds fall?

'Tis the Lord! O wondrous story!
'Tis the Lord, the King of glory!
At his feet we humbly fall;
Crown him, crown him Lord of all!

Have you any room for Jesus?

I wonder why there was no room for Mary, Joseph and the infant Christ at the first Christmas? No doubt it was a busy time, and accommodation space was at a premium, given on a first come, first served basis. Some no doubt very genuinely did not have any spare space which they could offer. Others perhaps did, but on seeing the expectant Mary, maybe they had second thoughts about turning their lodgings into a maternity ward ...

A bigger, and more pertinent question is: Why is it that many people have no room in their hearts and lives for Jesus today? No doubt many and varied answers could be given for this. For instance, in Luke 8:14 Jesus said that those 'choked by the cares and riches and pleasures of life' can thwart his Word from taking root and bearing fruit in their lives. In Mark 4:19 he put it slightly differently, mentioning 'the cares of the world, and the delight in riches and the desire for other things'. These 'fatal distractions' are around at Christmas as they are around all the year. We may have no room for the Christ of Christmas because he gets crowded out by the pressures upon us—the demands of friends and family, the need to earn a living, the enticements of modern advertising giving us the desire for the things of this passing world, etc. The immediate can seem far more pressing than the eternal. It is strange how at Christmas many can just celebrate celebrating, rather than celebrating the birth of Christ and the reason for his birth.

Our greatest need

Surely, though, the chief reason why people have no place for Jesus in their lives is that they just do not see their need of him: that they are sinners who need to be saved. Jesus himself said, 'Those who are well have no need of a physician, but those who are sick; I came not to call the righteous, but sinners' (Mark 2:17).

It was Martin Luther who said that 'An awareness of sin is the beginning of salvation.' Matthew 1:21 affirms, 'You shall call his name Jesus, for he will save his people from their sins.'

Just as we have no need of a torch on a summer's day, or an aspirin when we do not have a headache, or an ice cream on a cold winter's day at the seaside, unless the Holy Spirit of God convicts us of our sin and condemned plight, and then shows us that the Christ of Bethlehem who grew up to become the Christ of Calvary is God's own provision and answer to our need, we will never receive Christ as our own personal Saviour, and we will never rejoice in the salvation which he alone could procure at Calvary's cross.

So today, as throughout the centuries, many have no room for Christ. They have put up the 'No Vacancies' sign in the window of their hearts. Yet many also have been enabled to make room for Christ—and have even welcomed him in gladly. When they do so, they find that he takes over the whole house! When we know Christ, things are never the same again. 'But to all who received him, who believed in his name, he gave power to become children of God' (John 1:12).

Yes, when Christ is welcomed in, we receive God's own salvation: the forgiveness of our sins, peace with God, adoption into his family and the sure hope of eternal life. When we make room for him in our hearts, he prepares for us a room with him in heaven—an eternal home, more glorious than words can ever describe.

There was no room for Jesus at the first Christmas-time. The most important question of all today is: 'Have you any room for Jesus?'

Chapter 12

Have you any room for Jesus,
He who bore your load of sin?
As he knocks and asks admission,
Sinner, will you let him in?

Room for pleasure, room for business,
But for Christ the crucified,
Not a place that he can enter
In the heart for which he died?

Room for Jesus, King of Glory!
Hasten now his Word obey;
Swing the heart's door widely open,
Bid him enter while you may.

The Advent of our King

Christians who follow a church calendar sometimes point out that Christmas does not technically begin until sunset on 24 December. According to them, the weeks preceding Christmas are not Christmas but Advent. Somehow, I do not think that the shops have got their message!

The word 'Advent' means 'Coming'. It focuses our minds on the most stupendous fact of history: the coming of Christ into the world. Let us now consider the Advent of Christ from three angles:

God's eternal plan

Christ's coming into the world did not happen in a vacuum. No. The birth of Christ was part of the eternal plan of God. Christ's coming fulfilled the promises God had made beforehand: promises which we can read in the Scriptures.

At the dawn of time, when sin had marred God's perfect creation and our first ancestors, Adam and Eve, had become separated from their Maker, all seemed irreparably lost. But God intervened in grace! He promised a redeemer. Satan's work would be surely overthrown. In Genesis 3:15 God told of one of Eve's descendants who was to come. He would come, God said, and crush Satan's head. The promise was fulfilled when Christ was born of the Virgin Mary at Bethlehem. Genesis 3:15 is the earliest gospel promise; it's known as the *proto euangelion*. As the years continued, God revealed more details concerning the coming redeemer. Isaiah 7:14 showed that he would be born supernaturally of a virgin. Micah 5:2 told that he would be born in Bethlehem. Isaiah 53 revealed that his redeeming work would be accomplished by suffering on behalf of his people. Psalm 16 indicated that the redeemer would rise from the dead. Living after Christ's coming, we can see how all of these promises have been fulfilled to the letter in him. As only the omniscient and eternal God knows the end from the beginning, the fulfilment of prophecy is one of the many compelling evidences that the Bible is nothing less than the Word of God written.

God's eternal truth

Consider next the sober fact of Christ's coming. Galatians 4:4–5 reads: 'But when the time had fully come, God sent forth his Son, born of woman, born under the law, to redeem those who were under the law, so that we might receive adoption as sons.' We actually prove the reality of Christ's coming every time we write the date! Christ's birth divided time into BC (before Christ) and AD (*Anno Domino*, or 'year of our Lord'). We are living in the twenty-first century AD. In the first century AD none less than the eternal, ageless God was born! The infinite became an infant, the eternal entered into time and the Creator stepped into his creation. Our familiarity with the Christmas story must never blunt either the wonder or the mystery of the incarnation—that 'the Word became flesh and dwelt among us, full of grace and truth' (John 1:14). The reality of it all begs us to ask the reason for it. To this, the Bible gives a clear answer. SALVATION! The salvation of God's people: 'Christ Jesus came into the world to save sinners' (1 Timothy 1:15). 'For God sent the Son into the world, not to condemn the world, but that the world might be saved through him' (John 3:17). Christ's birth at Bethlehem, you see, was with a view to his death at Calvary. He was born to die, for it was on the cross that he wrought our eternal salvation, when he offered up himself as an eternal sacrifice for our sins. He, the sinless One, was condemned by God, so that we, the sinful ones, may be delivered from God's condemnation by faith in him. 'There is therefore now no condemnation for those who are in Christ Jesus' (Romans 8:1).

Christ's advent was long promised. Christ's advent was also a real fact of history, and a purposeful fact at that, integral to God's salvation plan. But thirdly, Advent also reminds us that:

Jesus is coming again!

Jesus is most certainly coming again. We are told that there are some 318 references in the Bible to the second coming of Christ. Christ's second coming is actually the goal of all history, and will be the most glorious, spectacular and unparalleled event ever. 'He shall come again in glory, to judge both the quick (living) and the dead', says an early Christian creed. The words are based on some of Christ's own words. He prophesied that, in a coming day 'they will see the Son of man coming on the clouds of heaven with power and great glory' (Matthew 24:30).

Mention of the second coming of Christ, of course, is very unsettling to those who do not belong to him—just as it warms the hearts of those who are his. The Christ of the Bible is revealed as a reigning, conquering Christ. He is coming again in glory! 'For he must reign until he has put all his enemies under his feet' (1 Corinthians 15:25).

So, are you ready for the second coming of Christ? He came, at the first Christmas, in fulfilment of the promises God made through his prophets. By his Spirit, he still comes: he comes and makes his home in human hearts when we confess our sin and cast ourselves upon him for mercy. But the Bible also tells us of the second coming of Christ, a coming that will be personal, visible, glorious and final, for 'the kingdom of this world has become the kingdom of our Lord and of his Christ, and he shall reign for ever and ever' (Revelation 11:15).

Advent, then—the weeks in the run-up to Christmas Day—fixes our attention on both the first and the second comings of the Lord Jesus Christ.

When came in flesh the incarnate Word,
The heedless world slept on,

And only simple shepherds heard
That God had sent his Son.

When comes the Saviour at the last,
From East to West shall shine
The awful pomp, and earth aghast
Shall tremble at the sign.

Lord, who could dare see thee descend
In state, unless he knew
Thou art the sorrowing sinner's friend,
The gracious and the true?

Dwell in our hearts, O Saviour blest;
So shall thine advent's dawn
'Twixt us and Thee, our bosom guest,
Be but the veil withdrawn.

Three Christmas paradoxes

For a few years now, I have had the benefit of a 'magic box of tricks' known as a PC—a personal computer. I recall that I almost ruptured myself carrying this PC home, but it has since proved its weight in gold. Being somewhat technologically illiterate, I have not got a clue how my PC works, but this does not stop me using it and benefiting from it. I can 'surf the net' for information, buy books 'online' and email friends in America and receive a reply from them the same day. (Formerly, a reply to an airmail would take about six weeks to receive.) Perhaps most of all, though, I use my PC as a word processor. This makes my old typewriter look very antique. The word processing facility enables me to write a document, save it, edit it, and, in principle, put a perfect copy of it all on a disk for the publisher. One wonders how the Puritans managed ...!

Do you know that Christmas is a little like my PC, in that, although there is much about Christmas that we do not understand, we can nevertheless rejoice in it and receive its benefits? Let me explain what I mean by drawing your attention to three of the mind-blowing paradoxes of Christmas.

1. The incarnation of Christ

The first Christmas paradox is that fact that, at the first Christmas, God became man. This is known as the 'incarnation': the enfleshment of God. 'The Word became flesh and dwelt among us' (John 1:14). It is an outstanding fact that in Jesus we have 'God in a body', for the Bible tells us that 'God is spirit' (John 4:24), that is, bodiless. Jesus, though, is literally 'Emmanuel, God with us', God with us in human flesh and form.

'Christ, the Son of God, became man, by taking to himself a true body, and a reasonable soul, being conceived by the power of the Holy Ghost, in the womb of the Virgin Mary, and born of her, yet without sin' (Westminster Shorter Catechism).

Jesus was and is God, yet the one person of Christ was and is man. The eternal Son of God became a Son of man at a particular moment in time. Both the deity and humanity of Christ are clearly evident from the Gospel records: he forgave sins, he calmed the stormy seas, he raised the dead—there is no doubt as to his deity. Yet he also experienced fatigue and thirst, he cried, and he bled and died. There is no doubt as to Christ's real humanity as well. It is a paradox which is beyond our comprehension. We will never understand it, yet we can rejoice in it, for at Christmas 'the Son of God became a Son of man that the sons of men might become the sons of God.'

2. The virgin birth of Christ

A second Christmas paradox is the fact that at the first Christmas, a virgin gave birth to a child. Elementary biology tells us that such things can't happen and such things don't happen. But the Bible affirms that it was the Virgin Mary who gave birth to the Lord Jesus on the first Christmas. Mary herself was understandably puzzled and perplexed as to how she could give birth whilst still in her virginity. The angel Gabriel informed her how the normal course of nature would be over-ridden by God himself: 'The Holy Spirit will come upon you, and the power of the Most High will overshadow you; therefore the child to be born will be called holy, the Son of God' (Luke 1:35).

Jesus had no human father. God was his Father. Hence he was conceived in a supernatural, not a natural way. Isaiah the prophet had predicted centuries previously: 'Behold, the virgin shall conceive and bear a son, and shall call his name Immanuel' (Isaiah 7:14, ESV).

The 'virgin birth of Christ' is one of the fundamental, non-negotiable tenets of the Christian faith. It is a vital truth, for if Jesus was the product of a mere human father, he would have inherited our human sin. But Jesus had to be sinless if he was to redeem the world from sin, by offering up his life as a sinless sacrifice for sinners. The Bible is thus as clear as to the virginal conception of Christ as it is of his sinlessness. For the Christian, it is easier to believe in the virgin birth of Christ than not to believe it, as it is so very much in-line with the whole of Christ's life. He entered the world supernaturally and he left the world supernaturally, and performed many supernatural acts in-between. Miracles present no difficulty to almighty God.

3. The death of Christ

A third Christmas paradox is that Jesus was born to die. He was born so that we might be born again. On the cross of Calvary, the living Saviour died, so that dying sinners might live. It is true to say that Christ accomplished far more by his death than by his life—even more than his teaching, miracles, and tender compassion to those around him. (Interestingly, the Bible commands us to remember specifically Christ's death, but not his birth. Christians partake of the Lord's Supper because Christ commanded us to remember him in this way. In the bread and wine of the Lord's Supper, the focus is on Calvary, not Bethlehem: Christ's redeeming death, not his marvellous life.)

'You shall call his name Jesus, for he will save his people from their sins' (Matthew 1:21). Jesus is the only Saviour for needy, condemned sinners like you and me. It was on the cross, thirty-three years after his miraculous birth, that Christ died a miraculous death. 'Christ died for our sins' (1 Corinthians 15:3). He suffered the just for the unjust, the sinless One on behalf of sinners. Paradoxically, it is Jesus' death which brings us new life, as his death is the only means by which our sins can be forgiven and our broken relationship with God restored. Jesus was born, not to live, but to die. There is new life for all who put their faith in the crucified Saviour, for 'the free gift of God is eternal life in Christ Jesus our Lord' (Romans 6:23).

So there are three Christmas paradoxes. We do not have the capacity to understand them fully. They transcend human reason. But that is no reason for not believing them, embracing them and enjoying them. It is the incarnate, virgin-born, Christ of Calvary who alone is the secret of a happy Christmas, a happy life and a happy eternity.

Christ, by highest heaven adored,
Christ, the everlasting Lord,
Late in time behold him come,
Offspring of a virgin's womb.
Veiled in flesh the Godhead see!
Hail the incarnate Deity!
Pleased as Man with men to dwell,
Jesus, our Immanuel

Hark! the herald angels sing
Glory to the new-born King.

Christmas: too good to be true?

For many of us, Christmas is and always has been a very exciting time of the year, and the anticipation and preparation are all part and parcel of the excitement.

If you were honest, though, do you think that this so-called 'season of good will' is actually too good to be true? I heard of one family, for instance, who are affected by internal strife and terrible arguments all the year round; but at Christmas-time they sink their differences, and have a strained sort of peace—only to resume their normal, war-like relationships as soon as Christmas is over.

Is that your suspicion too? Do you think that Christmas is nice but far removed from real life? Isn't it a time of make-believe—of fantasy, not reality, fiction not fact, with its jolly Father Christmas, sentimental children's nativity plays, fairy lights and all the rest which is a nice but momentary distraction from life in the raw …

It cannot be denied that much of what makes up a modern Christmas is man-made and not 'of God'. So much non-Christian 'clutter' has got bound up with this time of the year. It even comes as a shock to some when it is pointed out that there is no direct Biblical sanction which commands us to celebrate Christmas at all, and no Biblical evidence that the birth of Christ actually occurred on 25 December. Yet the core of Christmas is that the one true God, in his unfathomable love, has invaded our history in Jesus Christ and visited our planet 'for us and our salvation'. That fact cannot be denied. It is as true as the fact that you are alive at this moment. It was the birth of Christ which divided our calendar into BC and AD.

The witness of Luke

The first Christmas was no invention of a fertile imagination, but actually occurred at a certain time and in a certain place. Consider the opening verses of Luke's Gospel, which record it all. We have no reason why we should disbelieve what Luke wrote—he was a respected medical doctor and a careful historian. He wrote a painstakingly researched and matter of fact historical account of the life of Jesus, anxious that his readers would 'know the truth concerning the things of which you have been informed' (Luke 1:4). Luke was adamant as to the reality of the things he was writing and recording, and made a point of dating them against the background of the secular rulers of the time. He tells us (Luke 1:5) that Herod was king of Judea (a section of modern Israel) and that the emperor, Caesar Augustus, decreed that all should return to their place of birth and be enrolled for tax purposes (Luke 2:1). This meant that one young couple, Joseph and Mary, had to make the long journey to their home town of Bethlehem, and whilst there, Mary 'gave birth to her first-born son and wrapped him in swaddling cloths' (Luke 2:7); that is, whilst there, the Christ of Christmas was born—albeit in very humble, unflattering surroundings. There is no fiction or embellishment here!

The witness of John

Next, call in the evidence of the apostle John. We often read the opening verses of John's Gospel at Christmas-time, with its awesome statement and explanation that 'the Word became flesh and dwelt among us, full of grace and truth' (John 1:14). John started out his career in the fishing business. If you had seen any fishermen on the Sea of Galilee, you would have known what down to earth, if not rough and ready, characters they were. Yet you could not persuade John that Jesus and his transforming love were anything but real. The reality of the Christ who was born at Christmas comes out especially in the opening verses of a letter which John wrote many years after he had first encountered Christ. He opened this letter in this way: 'That which was from the beginning, which we have heard, which we have seen with our eyes, which we have looked upon and touched with our hands concerning the word of life [Jesus]—the life was made manifest, and we saw it, and testify to it, and proclaim to you the eternal life which was with the Father and was made manifest to us ... (1 John 1:1–2).

Yes, John had heard, seen and actually touched the eternal Son of God—the Jesus Christ of Christmas. His senses did not deceive him.

The evidence of the millions

Finally, what of the millions today, and the millions in the last two thousand years or so, who can testify, with hand on heart, that Jesus and his salvation are real? They owe their all to him, and have found that he is the key to life and that his saving love has made an infinity of difference to them. How has he made such a difference? The message of Christmas gives us the answer.

At the first Christmas, an angel from heaven explained to Joseph about the baby to whom Mary was to give birth: 'You shall call his name Jesus, for he will save his people from their sins' (Matthew 1:21). It is here that we reach the heart of the matter, namely, knowing Christ as our Saviour. The Christ who was born at Bethlehem was born to be the Saviour of sinners. 'We have seen and testify that the Father has sent his Son as the Saviour of the world' (1 John 4:14). How did the Christ born at Bethlehem become our Saviour? He accomplished the salvation of his people thirty-three years after his birth when he died on the cross of Calvary. He was born to die. The cross overshadowed his cradle. Who would ever invent an old rugged cross and a crucified God? The birth of Christ and the death of Christ were both realer than real. The explanation for the crucified Christ is his Saviour-hood. The apostle Peter declared that 'he himself bore our sins in his body on the tree' (1 Peter 2:24). That is, Christ paid the punishment that should have been paid by lost, condemned sinners, so that all who believe in him may be forever freed from God's condemnation and, knowing God's gracious pardon for their sins, may be at peace with their Maker for time and eternity.

Christmas, then, is real and not make-believe. The evidence for it is all there in the Word of God, the Bible, and in the life of every single Christian who has experienced the saving grace of God in Jesus Christ. The Christ of Christmas is for real. He is a real Saviour, who saves real people, from a real hell, for a real heaven, and bestows a real, wonderful and lasting salvation. The question is, Do you believe that Christ and his salvation are really real? Do you know Christ personally, or do you just know a bit about him? If you are a stranger to Christ, what better time than Christmas to begin with God? If you have never done so before, ask the God of heaven to reveal himself to you. Read his Word, the Bible. Invite the Lord Jesus into your life, trusting that he died in your place and for your sins when he died on the cross. Receive the gift of salvation that God offers you freely, but at such a cost, in Jesus Christ. Knowing the Christ of Christmas means that you will be able to sing the Christmas carols with sincerity and joy, and begin to walk with God day by day for the rest of your life here, and your life hereafter there.

'Happy Christmas!' We often hear the words, but are unsure just how to define a happy Christmas. A truly happy Christmas is a Christ-centred Christmas. Knowing the reality of his presence make all the difference both to Christmas and to the unknown, uncertain days ahead.

When giving is getting

In Acts 20:35 we have some words of Jesus which are not recorded for us in the Gospel records. They are quoted by the apostle Paul: 'remembering the words of the Lord Jesus, how he said, "It is more blessed to give than to receive."' How Paul came to know this saying we don't know. He possibly came to know the saying from one of the disciples who was acquainted with the Lord Jesus' ministry on earth. Paul's conversion occurred after Jesus' earthly ministry, so it is unlikely that he would have given much attention to Jesus and his teaching while their earthly lives coincided.

'It is more blessed to give than to receive.' Do you have an inkling of what this means? Can you recall some happiness you gained by what you gave away? There is the joy we see in children's eyes at Christmas-time when we give them just the present they were hoping for. But there is also the joy of giving more intangible things. Don't underestimate the joy which you can give when you send your sincere Christmas greetings to someone. Proverbs 12:25 tells us that 'anxiety in a man's heart weighs him down, but a good word makes him glad'. Then there is the happiness of giving yourself—your time and availability—to others when they are in need. In many ways, this is more costly than a cheque which takes a mere minute or so to write. Remember that you can do what an expensive machine cannot do. Remember too that whilst one person cannot change the whole world, you can change the whole world for one person, just by your love, concern, availability, presence and prayers. 'It is more blessed to give than to receive.' That suggests that giving is actually getting. In Luke 6:38 Jesus said, 'Give, and it will be given to you; good measure, pressed down, shaken together, running over, will be put into your lap.' Proverbs 11:24 tells us that 'one man gives freely, yet grows all the richer;

another withholds what he should give, and only suffers want'. Proverbs 11:25 says that 'a liberal man will be enriched, and one who waters will himself be watered'.

The giving God

At the heart of Christmas—and the sometimes forgotten meaning behind the giving and receiving of Christmas presents—lies the fact of the God who gave. John 3:16 summarises Christmas as it summarises the Christian faith when it states: 'God so loved the world that he gave his only Son, that whoever believes in him should not perish but have eternal life.' In Galatians 2:20 we read of 'the Son of God who loved me and gave himself for me'.

Gifts tell us something about both the giver and the receiver. What then of this, the greatest gift? The recipients, John 3:16 tells us, are in peril. They are in danger of perishing in hell, under God's eternal judgement, had not God graciously intervened, and given his Son to die for their sins and so bestow on them eternal life instead of the eternal death which they deserve because of their sin. The gift of God's Son tells us about both the heart of God the Giver and our own hearts. We are needy, condemned sinners, but God in Christ is a gracious Saviour. The measure of God's grace is the measure of his gift. Romans 8:32 reminds us: 'He who did not spare his own Son but gave him up for us all, will he not also give us all things with him?'

Blessed be God, our God!
Who gave for us his well-beloved Son,
The gift of gifts, all other gifts in one—
Blessed be God, our God.

What will he not bestow,
Who freely gave this mighty gift unbought,

Unmerited, unheeded, and unsought—
What will he not bestow?

He spared not his Son!
'Tis this that silences each rising fear;
'Tis this that bids the hard thought disappear—
He spared not his Son!

The greatest gift

So thank God for the greatest gift: 'the free gift of God is eternal life in Christ Jesus our Lord' (Romans 6:23). Salvation, according to the Bible, is a gift to be received. It is this which distinguishes the faith of the Bible. All the world's man-made religions are characterised by what we are meant to do for God—as though we could give the all-sufficient One anything! The stress of the Bible, though, is that salvation is by God's grace—God's loving and giving of Jesus to needy sinners to be their Saviour. We cannot give anything to God. Finite creatures can never put the infinite Creator in their debt. He is our Maker and Sustainer. We are totally dependent on him. We are sinners; hence, in our natural, Christless state, even our best gifts to him are tainted and abhorrent to him. Yet the message of Christmas is that God in Christ has reached out in grace and mercy to us: giving, restoring and making us glad. 'In Christ God was reconciling the world to himself, not counting their trespasses against them, and entrusting to us the message of reconciliation' (2 Corinthians 5:19).

It is indeed blessed to be able to give. The God of the Bible gave and still gives. What can we give him? Nothing. Yet, paradoxically, and amazingly, our receiving his greatest gift brings joy to his heart.

What can I give him,
Poor as I am?

Chapter 16

If I were a shepherd,
I would bring a lamb;
If I were a wise man,
I would do my part;
Yet what I can I give him:
Give my heart.

Happy Hanukkah!

The feast of Hanukkah

If you have any Jewish friends, you might like to send them a card around Christmas-time and wish them a 'Happy Hanukkah'.

Hanukkah is mentioned just once in the Bible—in John 10:22–23, where it is referred to as the 'feast of the Dedication'. This happy festival commemorates the restoration and rededication of the temple in Jerusalem in 165 BC. The pagan armies of Antiochus Epiphanes had taken Jerusalem by storm, and defiled the temple, bringing their idols into it and even offering a pig on the altar. The Jewish people were understandably and righteously irate. Under the leadership of Judas Maccabeus, they rose up, drove out the foreign army and regained possession of their holy temple. The feast of Dedication—Hanukkah—was instituted to commemorate this deliverance and victory.

The Hanukkah candle

Did you know that Jewish people light a special, nine-branched candle at Hanukkah? Why? Well, the story goes that in 165 BC, after the priests had cleansed the temple after Antiochus Epiphanes' ravages, they were about to light the seven-branched candle on the lampstand in the Holy Place. They found, though, that they only had a small cruse of oil. The problem was that this specially-refined oil for the temple lamp took eight days to prepare. What could they do? Well, they lit the lamp with the oil they had and prepared some new oil. Jewish legend then says that a miracle occurred. Almighty God provided a miraculous supply so that the temple light did not run out of oil during the week whilst the new oil was being prepared. The temple light was thus kept burning miraculously, right until the time when the new oil arrived.

Hanukkah, then, is a happy feast for those who celebrate it. It commemorates a deliverance from oppression, and it is celebrated as a 'Feast of Lights'. The Feast lasts for eight days, and a special, nine branched Hanukkah candle is lit, beginning with the main light or 'servant.'

Hanukkah and Christmas

It seems more than an 'undesigned coincidence' that the Jewish festival of Hanukkah and the Christian festival of Christmas are celebrated more or less at the same time each year. The respective feasts coincide. When Jewish people are celebrating a divine intervention in their nation's history, Christians are celebrating a divine intervention in world history. At Christmas, Christian celebrate the incarnation of God—how 'the Word became flesh and dwelt among us, full of grace and truth' (John 1:14).

Deliverance lies at the heart of Hanukkah, and an even greater deliverance lies at the heart of Christmas. This deliverance was wrought by the Great Deliverer or Saviour: 'Christ Jesus came into the world to save sinners' (1 Timothy 1:15).

Notice why Christ came. He came *to save*. He came to deliver. 'You shall call his name Jesus, for he will save his people from their sins (Matthew 1:21)..

Under Judas Maccabeus, the Jewish religion was saved from dying a death. Remarkably, though, Jesus saved his people by dying a death. His birth was with a view to his death, as his cradle was with a view to his cross. His incarnation was with a view to his propitiation—with a view towards turning the wrath of God against sinners aside. This he did when he died at Calvary, for it was on the cross that he wrought our deliverance when he 'gave himself for our sins to deliver us from the present evil age, according to the will of our God and Father' (Galatians 1:4).

At Christmas, then, a mighty Deliverer was born. It is by Jesus alone that we can be delivered from the penalty and power of sin. Jesus alone can save us from the wrath of God. Jesus alone can turn us around from heading to the city of destruction and direct our steps towards the glorious city of God.

The festival of light

We have seen how Hanukkah is a festival of lights. The Hanukkah candle is lit and displayed at this happy feast. But Christmas too is a festival of light when we have come to know the Christ of Christmas.

None of us feel very at home in the dark. Darkness speaks of danger, depression, the unknown, fear, and, according to the Bible, the wrath of God. But Jesus is the light of the world. His light banishes our spiritual darkness. Jesus said, 'I am the light of the world. He who follows me will not walk in darkness but will have the light of life' (John 8:12). In John 12:46, Jesus said, 'I have come as light into the world, that whoever believes in me may not remain in darkness.' All who believe in Jesus escape from the outer darkness of hell. Why? Because on the cross Jesus, the 'Light of the World', took the darkness of hell and the wrath of God, so that by believing in him we may be delivered from the dominion of darkness and enjoy God's light and love forever.

How fitting then that Hanukkah and Christmas are celebrated at the same time. Hanukkah is a joyful time for Jewish people, commemorating a deliverance. In the Christ of Christmas, though, we have an even greater deliverance. In Jesus we have eternal salvation. He is the light of the world. By his redeeming work we will dwell forever in God's eternal light.

I heard the voice of Jesus say,
'I am this dark world's Light;
Look unto me, thy morn shall rise,
And all thy days be bright.'
I looked to Jesus, and I found
In him my Star, my Sun;

And in that light of life I'll walk
Till travelling days are done.

Christmas: God's humanity, poverty and agony

I am ashamed to confess that in the past, once or twice, the arrival of Christmas caught me almost by surprise. Most years I have to work right up until Christmas Eve, and there is also the enjoyable responsibility of preparing Christmas messages. I, as much as anyone, am in danger of getting carried along by the general Christmas 'hype', and missing out on the very best; that is, failing to take adequate time out to ponder the wonder of Christmas—the wonder of the incarnation; the fact that God became man and entered into our world in the Lord Jesus Christ. It has been well said that 'If you are just too busy for private devotions, you are just too busy.' Personally, I would encourage every Christian to get up earlier during Christmas week, and give the accounts of the birth of Christ a good, careful and prayerful read.

When we rewind the clock two thousand years or so to the first Christmas, what do we find actually happened of such great importance? Actually, we can summarise the message of Christmas in three words. The Bible tells us that, at the first Christmas, in love and mercy, God took upon himself three things: humanity, poverty and agony.

1. The humanity of God

At the first Christmas, God took upon himself humanity. 'The Word became flesh and dwelt among us, full of grace and truth' (John 1:14). 'Since therefore the children share in flesh and blood, he himself likewise partook of the same nature ...' (Hebrews 2:14). Yes, at the first Christmas, the infinite God was 'contracted to a span' and 'incomprehensibly made man'. Paul wrote of Christ that 'in him the whole fulness of deity dwells bodily' (Colossians 2:9). Why was this so? As the Nicene Creed says, 'for us men and for our salvation he came down from heaven, and was incarnate by the Holy Ghost of the Virgin Mary, and was made man'.

The immortal God cannot die. The God who is infinite Spirit (John 4:24) had no flesh and blood. In Jesus Christ, however, God became man, so that he could die on a cross and so pay the death penalty for our sins. Unless Christ's cross overshadows Christ's cradle, we will soon lose the true meaning of Christmas. We shall get lost in a mere seasonal sentimentality, and be no different, wiser or spiritually enriched once Christmas has ended. In Jesus, God, in the second Person of the Trinity, became a real flesh and blood man; and on the cross, thirty-three years or so after the first Christmas, shed his precious blood so that we might be able to enjoy God's free gift of forgiveness and eternal life.

2. The poverty of God

At the first Christmas, God took upon himself poverty. 2 Corinthians 8:9 reads, 'For you know the grace of our Lord Jesus Christ, that though he was rich, yet for your sake he became poor, so that by his poverty you might become rich.' This was certainly so. In Luke 9:58 Jesus testified, 'Foxes have holes and birds of the air have nests; but the Son of man has nowhere to lay his head.' Jesus left the glory of heaven for the poverty of earth. Jesus left the land unsullied by sin and unmarred by sorrow, for this sin-scarred earth, with all its pain, poverty, rejection and misunderstanding. The contrast between the pre-incarnate and the incarnate state of Christ just cannot be measured. But his taking upon himself poverty, when he was born in that lowly stable, was to make us rich indeed –rich in a spiritual sense with those 'solid joys and lasting treasures which none but Zion's children know'.

3. The agony of God

At the first Christmas, God not only took upon himself humanity and poverty, but also agony as well.

Out of the ivory palaces,
Into a world of woe,
Only his great, eternal love
Made my Saviour go.

If you are acquainted with the Gospel records, you will know that God in Christ is no stranger to suffering. He actually experienced everything we dread and more: rejection, misunderstanding, betrayal, denial, hunger, thirst, fatigue and pain. In Jesus, God took upon himself agony—an agony which was to reach its climax at the cross of Calvary, when the sinless Christ was 'made sin' for us, and punished by God in our place, so that in indescribable agony he cried out, 'My God, my God, why hast thou forsaken me?' (Matthew 27:46).

Amidst the surface Christmas jollity, there is always the danger of forgetting that the agony of Christ on the cross is actually the reason for the season of Christmas. The message of Christmas is the message of the Bible, which is the message of the gospel, summarised in 2 Corinthians 5:19: that 'in Christ God was reconciling the world to himself, not counting their trespasses against them'. God and sinners reconciled! That truly is salvation. The gospel is the gospel of reconciliation: we 'rejoice in God through our Lord Jesus Christ, through whom we have now received our reconciliation' (Romans 5:11).

The question then is begged both at Christmas-time and all the time: Have you been reconciled to God your Maker by Christ? Have you put your faith in the One who was born at Bethlehem to save you? Have you received the gift of God which is eternal life in Christ Jesus our Lord? The Christ who was born at Bethlehem is the Christ who suffered at Calvary and is the Christ who is alive today and will one day take his people to be with him for ever. Beware of the danger of being too busy at Christmas-time, and remember that Jesus is the reason for the season.

Hail, the heaven-born Prince of Peace!
Hail, the Sun of Righteousness!
Lift and life to all he brings,
Risen with healing in his wings.
Mild he lays his glory by,
Born that man no more may die,
Born to raise the sons of earth,
Born to give them second birth.

Hark! the herald angels sing
Glory to the new-born King.

Just according to plan

I once met a fellow who told me that he did not enjoy Christmas at all. When I asked why, I thought that he would give me some sort of religious objection, but his reply was nothing of the sort. He said that Christmas left him exhausted. Christmas, he said, only 'works' if it goes according to plan. Deadlines have to be met, he went on: letters posted by a certain day, parcels by another day, rooms ready and beds made in time for the relatives' arrival, turkeys in the oven by a certain time ... No wonder that he collapses in a heap on the sofa on Christmas afternoon!

You will be glad to know that the first Christmas went exactly to plan—according to the divine plan of the God whose purposes cannot be thwarted or frustrated. The Bible tells us that 'when the time had fully come, God sent forth his Son, born of woman, born under the law' (Galatians 4:4). That expression 'when the time had fully come', I am told, is a metaphor of year being added to year, like an unfilled measure, filled drop by drop, until the complete fulness came. The expression has also been translated as 'when the time was ripe'.

The fulness of time

Jesus was sent at just the right time. If you know your history, you will know that world conditions in the first century were never riper for the spread of the gospel: there were synagogues in almost every town, which gave an ideal 'platform' for the gospel; they had the common Greek language; they had the Roman roads and ships, and the Roman army kept a degree of peace and stability. If you know your Bible, you will know that in the Old Testament God had made many promises to send the Messiah. And if you know your own heart, you will know just how undone you would be if God had not sent his Son to be your Saviour. We are all sinners. We need to be saved. In the fulness of time, God sent the Saviour we so desperately need. 'We have seen and testify that the Father has sent his Son as the Saviour of the world' (1 John 4:14).

Yes, the first Christmas went exactly according to God's plan. Way back, in Old Testament times—some eight hundred years before Jesus was born—the prophet Isaiah prophesised: 'For to us a child is born, to us a son is given; and the government will be upon his shoulder, and his name will be called "Wonderful Counsellor, Mighty God, Everlasting Father, Prince of Peace"' (Isaiah 9:6). Who else but the Lord Jesus fulfils this prophecy? He is the child that was born, He is the Son that was given. In Jesus, God became man; in Jesus, the eternal entered into time, leaving heaven for earth, so that we might leave earth for heaven if we put our faith in him.

The right time and place

The first Christmas also went exactly to plan with regard to the actual place of Christ's birth. Again, some eight hundred years BC, Almighty God, through the prophet Micah foretold that Christ would be born in Bethlehem. 'But you, O Bethlehem Ephrathah, who are little to be among the clans of Judah, from you shall come forth for me one who is to be ruler in Israel, whose origin is from of old, from ancient days [or 'from everlasting']' (Micah 5:2). But there appeared to be a hitch in the divine plans! Joseph and Mary were living in Nazareth, in the north of Israel, a long way from Bethlehem in the south. But nothing was too difficult for God. He ruled and over-ruled, and made the Roman emperor of the day decree that all should go back to their town of origin and be enrolled for taxation purposes. So we read in the Bible how 'Joseph ... went up from Galilee, from the city of Nazareth, to Judea, to the city of David, which is called Bethlehem ... and while they were there, the time came for her [Mary] to be delivered. And she gave birth to her first-born son ...' (Luke 2:4–7).

The death of Christ—according to plan

So the birth of Christ went just according to plan. This being so, was it not a shame that the One born at Bethlehem came to such an awful end, when thirty-three years later he was nailed to a cross, and hung up to bleed and die an ignominious death? Had not God lost control? Had not his eternal plan been ruined? No. Even the death of Christ by the hands of wicked man was exactly according to God's plan. Acts 2:23 informs us that 'this Jesus, delivered up according to the definite plan and foreknowledge of God, you crucified by the hands of lawless men'.

The death of Jesus, exactly like the birth of Jesus, was no mere accident but a certain divine appointment. Jesus was born to die. His reason for living was his dying. He had to bleed and die to be able to save you and me, as the Bible says that 'the wages of sin is death' (Romans 6:23) and 'without the shedding of blood there is no forgiveness of sins' (Hebrews 9.22). Indeed, we can say categorically, that unless the cross overshadows the cradle in our thinking, we have lost the true meaning and purpose of Christmas.

Our God reigns!

So take heart that it is Almighty God who rules this world. He is on the throne. No matter what the turmoil, he is still in control. He is the God who knows the end from the beginning and his purposes cannot be defeated. And if you are saved, that is, if you belong to Jesus, it is because God chose you in Christ even before the foundation of the world (Ephesians 1:4), so careful and sure are his plans for your eternal blessing. And if you do not believe in Jesus, what better time than now, at Christmas-time, to trust him as your Saviour and so receive the greatest gift you can ever receive. 'The free gift of God is eternal life in Christ Jesus our Lord' (Romans 6:23).

'I wish it could be Christmas every day'

When Christmas comes around again, the shops and supermarkets always seem to blast out the same old tunes over the tannoy. These aren't everyone's cup of tea, but I confess that I rather like them. One of these songs—a song which originated back in the 1970s—has the chorus 'I wish it could be Christmas every day.' I heard on the news that one fellow in the West of England took this literally. In seeking to combat his depression, he made sure that, for him, it was a kind of Christmas every day. Included in this was treating himself to a full Christmas dinner every day of the year—a practice which gained him quite a few stones of excess weight.

Truth be told, for Christians it really is Christmas every day. For whilst we enjoy the season of Christmas, with its Bible readings and carols which focus on Christ's incarnation, the heart of the Christmas message, with its immense blessing, is with us all year around, and not just at Christmas-time. Christmas comes and goes all too quickly. But the joy of the Lord remains with us.

Did you know that God commands us to be joyful? In Philippians 4:4 we are enjoined, 'Rejoice in the Lord always; again I will say, Rejoice.' That is what we are to do: 'Rejoice in the Lord'. It reminds us that the first Christmas had the message of 'good news of a great joy' (Luke 2:10). At Christmas time—and every day of the year—we have just cause to rejoice in the Lord, in his humanity, his deity and his potency.

1. The humanity of the Lord

We rejoice in the humanity of the Lord, for at Christmas-time, God became man. 'The Word became flesh and dwelt among us, full of grace and truth' (John 1:14). In Christ, the eternal God identified himself with our humanity. Our God knows what it is like to be human, for in Christ he shared our human lot, apart from sin. God in Christ was born, lived and walked this earth. He knew and experienced the stresses and strains of family life; he knows the stresses and strains of the life of work; he experienced hostility and difficulty; he experienced disappointment and sorrow; he experienced rejection and physical pain. Christ is no stranger to intense physical, mental, psychological and spiritual distress. In Christ we have a Saviour of the utmost sympathy. 'For we have not a high priest who is unable to sympathise with our weaknesses, but one who in every respect has been tempted as we are, yet without sin' (Hebrews 4:15).

2. The deity of the Lord

Christians also rejoice in Christ's deity both at Christmas-time and all the time. Do you remember the angel's words to the virgin Mary? She was told, much to her shock and amazement: 'Behold, you will conceive in your womb and bear a son, and you shall call his name Jesus' (Luke 1:31). But then the angel expanded on the identity of this special baby: 'He will be great, and will be called the Son of the Most High; and the Lord God will give to him the throne of his father David, and he will reign over the house of Jacob for ever; and of his kingdom there will be no end' (Luke 1:32–33).

In Jesus, then, we are dealing with God. He is the Son of God and God the Son, to be worshipped along with the Father and the Holy Spirit. One of the earliest Christian creeds was simply 'Jesus is Lord'. We rejoice in this Lord: the Lord who is now enthroned in heaven, seated at the right hand of God. We rejoice that this King is coming to reign and will soon bring all things under his sway. We rejoice that Jesus reigns, and that Jesus shall reign and bring in his eternal kingdom of righteousness and peace. Christians, then, are always in worshipful wonder of the Christ who came at Christmas. We are in wonder of his glorious Person. He is the God-man, fully human and fully divine. But also, at Christmas-time and all the time, we rejoice in:

3. The potency of the Lord

In Christ we have the all-sufficient Saviour for our deepest need. 'You shall call his name Jesus, for he will save his people from their sins' (Matthew 1:21). 'To you is born this day in the city of David a Saviour, who is Christ the Lord' (Luke 2:11). 'The Son of man came to seek and to save the lost' (Luke 19:10).

Christians always rejoice in Christ's saving potency. He alone can save. It is only through Jesus—the one born at Christmas and the one who died and was raised at Easter—that we can be sure that our sins are forgiven and we have peace with God and so may enjoy God's friendship and fellowship for all eternity. 'He is able for all time to save those who draw near to God through him, since he always lives to make intercession for them' (Hebrews 7:25).

The salvation which Christ wrought is a salvation to be enjoyed at Christmas-time, in all the ups and downs of the coming year, and for all eternity. 'The free gift of God is eternal life in Christ Jesus our Lord' (Romans 6:23).

Jesus is a potent Saviour. He has raised us up from spiritual death. He has bestowed on us the gift of eternal life—that blessed fellowship with God which is our chief end and for which we were designed. It's incomparable; it's a joy which cannot stop when Christmas ends.

For the Christian, then, it truly is 'Christmas every day'. For no matter what our lot in this life is, we have been enabled to rejoice in the Lord and all his benefits. The blessing of our unchanging, unchangeable Saviour is a blessing which this world cannot give, and a blessing which this world cannot take away. In knowing Jesus it is Christmas every day!

The transfiguration of the ordinary

As is well known, the original Christmas message was broadcast from heaven to earth, by an angel to some shepherds, as the latter were going about their normal occupation in the fields surrounding Bethlehem. They were on the night shift, just going about their usual routine when the great message came to them: 'To you is born this day in the city of David a Saviour, who is Christ the Lord' (Luke 2:11). On going over to Bethlehem, those nameless shepherds found that it was indeed so. They found the infant Christ lying in a manger. Mary and Joseph were, of course, there too, and so the shepherds related to them the details of the angelic visitation they had just had: how they had come to know about the birth of the Saviour, the promised Christ who is God in the flesh. After this momentous, unforgettable event in the shepherds' lives, though, you might wonder what exactly happened to them? What did they do next? Luke tells us what they did next. In Luke 2:20 he says, 'the shepherds returned'. That is, they went back to their normal world of work: their allotted, unglamorous task of caring for sheep. But Luke also adds a significant detail when he expands: 'the shepherds returned, glorifying and praising God for all they had heard and seen, as it had been told them' (Luke 2:20).

Making the ordinary extraordinary

The shepherds' returning to their normal lives after their encounter with Christ has a message for us. In their story we can see a mixture of the human and the divine, the heavenly and the earthly, the ordinary and the extraordinary. In a nutshell, we can see how an encounter with Christ transforms and transfigures, and yet, paradoxically, certain things remain the same. Think of it. The shepherds had actually met the very Son of God and promised Messiah. They would never be the same again ... yet they went back to the same jobs they had been doing before. Their job remained the same: they wore the same clothes, in the same place, and used the same tools of the trade. We can speculate that they also went back to the same homes, ate similar meals, and lived through many of the ups and downs, highs and lows, joys, sorrows and frustrations which make up all of our lives in this world. The shepherds' circumstances were the same. Yet, paradoxically, they were not the same because, having met the Christ of God, the shepherds were now not the same. Having encountered the one and only Saviour, they would always view the world from a different perspective.

The Saviour who makes all the difference

But what about all this in relation to the Christmases which we experience? What about us when we go back to our normal routines after the excitement and hype of the so-called 'festive season'? If all we take back with us are memories of a 'merry', secular Christmas—meals with friends, useful presents, TV specials, etc—truth be told, we have gained nothing really lasting from Christmas. There is an infinite, qualitative difference between celebrating Christmas and celebrating the Christ of Christmas. For the Christian, the joy of Christmas is an all-year-round joy, even an eternal joy. There is the wonder of the incarnation—that God should actually become man for our salvation; there is the wonder of the reason for it all—that in infinite mercy God should actually send his Son to be our Saviour; there is the joy of salvation, for the babe of Bethlehem grew up to be the Christ of Calvary, and on the cross Christ shed his blood so that we may have the forgiveness of sins, peace with God, and the sure hope of eternal life. These are all blessings which never fade. The tinsel is eventually taken down, the tree is put out for the dustmen to collect, and the worn, torn and out-of-date *Radio Times* is put with the papers for recycling. We ourselves return to work, and struggle with all the battles and handicaps which threaten to pull us down ... But the joy of the Lord and the presence of the Lord remain and will for ever remain with us. 'I will never fail you nor forsake you' (Hebrews 13:5). 'For I am sure that neither death, nor life, ... nor things present, nor things to come, ... nor anything else in all creation, will be able to separate us from the love of God in Christ Jesus our Lord (Romans 8:38–39).

In 2 Corinthians 5:17 we read, 'Therefore, if any one is in Christ he is a new creation; the old has passed away, behold, the new has come.' The shepherds of Bethlehem would say 'Amen' to that. They were never the same again, once they had met the Saviour. They went back to their normal work, for sure, yet they went 'glorifying and praising God'.

Thank God that his grace reaches ordinary individuals, who do ordinary jobs and live in ordinary houses. Thank God that his extraordinary, saving grace reaches ordinary people like you and me. The grace of heaven comes down to people like us—but we are not in heaven yet. We are both 'in Christ' and yet very much bound to life on earth as well. Knowing the Christ of Bethlehem, though, makes and will make an eternity of difference. Knowing him is the difference between alienation from God and reconciliation to him; eternal salvation or eternal loss; spending eternity in heaven or spending eternity in hell. The Christ of Christmas is a Christ who can be known, here and now. He still 'receives sinners and eats with them' (Luke 15:2). He is the extraordinary Saviour who makes such a qualitative difference to us, whoever and wherever we are. May the true Christmas joy then—the joy of knowing Christ—be yours, now and always.

Joy to the world! the Lord is come!
Let earth receive her King;

Let every heart prepare him room,
And heaven and nature sing.

No more let sins and sorrows grow,
Nor thorns infest the ground;
He comes to make his blessings flow
Far as the curse is found.

He rules the world with truth and grace,
And makes the nations prove
The glories of his righteousness,
The wonders of his love.

Soli Deo Gloria

The reason for the season

It's Christmas time, it's that time of the year
For parties and families and seasonal cheer.
But behind it all, lies Christ's Incarnation,
For God became man, to procure our salvation.
'The Word became flesh' for sinful women and men
And came as a baby to old Bethlehem.
Father Christmas, in truth, is only a fable;
The gospel is true: God was born in that stable.
The story is greater than mere tongue can tell;
The wonder of wonders—Immanuel.
God loved the world so, that his own Son he gave;
Christ Jesus came, for us sinners to save.
Three and thirty years later, on an old rugged tree,
Christ died for sinners, at dark Calvary.
There on that cross, he did shed his own blood
To reconcile sinners, like us, back to God.
In him alone we are sure we're forgiven;
By him alone have we right to God's heaven.
Be most careful, then, of mere frivolous mirth,
And ponder the reason why Christ came to earth;
Unless that old cross overshadows the manger,
To God's own grace you will just be a stranger.
Christmas Day's coming—but soon it is past;
Yet the blessing of Christ for eternity lasts.
Apart from God's mercy you surely are lost;
Give thanks for that baby—give thanks for the cross.

TJEC